B*tch Don't Kill My Vibe

How To Stop Worrying, End
Negative Thinking, Cultivate
Positive Thoughts, And Start
Living Your Best Life

REESE OWEN

ALL BOOKS BY REESE OWEN

Check out my other ebooks,
paperback books, and audiobooks
available on Amazon and Audible:

B*tch Don't Kill My Vibe
How To Stop Worrying, End Negative Thinking,
Cultivate Positive Thoughts,
And Start Living Your Best Life

Just Do The Damn Thing
How To Sit Your @ss Down Long Enough To
Exert Willpower, Develop Self Discipline,
Stop Procrastinating, Increase Productivity,
And Get Sh!t Done

Make Your Brain Your B*tch
Mental Toughness Secrets To Rewire Your Mindset
To Be Resilient And Relentless, Have Self Confidence
In Everything You Do,
And Become The Badass You Truly Are

REESE OWEN

Since you're my friend—we're friends, right??—I'd like to give you my audiobook (~~usually $14.95~~) for **FREE**.

Search for my name
"Reese Owen" on Audible.

Audible member? Use a credit.
New to Audible? Get this audiobook **free** with your free trial.

REESE OWEN

CONTENTS

Part 4: This Is The Only Part That Actually Has A Name—The New You…Woo-Hoo!

INTRODUCTION

Welcome to the first step of the rest of your life. Hopefully, with the help of this book, it won't be quite so miserable from here on out. Or maybe your life is already perfect. In which case, you should write a book. If you're like most people who have ~~shitty~~ not so perfect lives, read on so I can talk you off the ledge. Maybe, just maybe, you can learn from my friend Joe, a man who has spent his entire existence hopelessly running around in figurative circles. He is a perfectly ordinary guy, just like you, or me. He just has a lot going on inside his head at any given moment. Just like you and me. He can't seem to get a grip on life and is always falling behind.

His morning begins in the same way every day. The ~~annoying ass~~ alarm is going off and he turns his sleepy eyes to the source of the noise only to realize that, yet

1

again, he is already late for work. (And you can probably guess how he feels about his job.) He talks to himself saying, "Man, I don't want to go to work today," and begrudgingly gets out of bed. He doesn't even have to imagine, because he already knows what kind of day it will be. He stumbles across the room to the closet to rummage through the unfolded heap of clothes. No time to shower, he thinks to himself, it's not like anyone would notice if I did. He wants to go back to sleep and quit his job, but he knows that everything depends on that paycheck.

He's ready to go hop on the bicycle, something he used to love doing, but now is only a means of taking him from Point A that he doesn't want to be at, to Point B that he doesn't want to be at. There is no leisure in it anymore. This used to be fun. The ride to work is no longer interesting so he just looks straight ahead and doesn't take notice of what is around him.

He gets to the office and the receptionist is there at the front desk as always, giving him a disapproving look. He imagines that what she's thinking might be something like, "Lazy-ass Joe, late again. Didn't even have time to brush your hair, or iron your shirt, or at least pick out a shirt that doesn't have a grease stain on it from the gas station chili cheese dogs you binged on in your room alone last night because you don't have any friends because nobody likes you because you suck. Now we all have to look at…that…all day." Yeah. That's probably exactly what she's thinking.

Tired, disheveled, wrinkly, greasy Joe shuffles into his ~~office~~ shared cubicle, does his job and works hard on his project, only to be told that his work isn't good enough. He'll have to do it over again, but faster this time since it should be completed before the end of the day. I'll never get this done by five. He spends so much time worrying that in an instant, it is already time to go home.

The project goes unfinished and is left to pick up tomorrow, at which point he'll be even further behind. As he is leaving work, he is approached by a female co-worker who wants to go out for a drink or a bite to eat with him. It's Abby from Accounting. Looks like she finally noticed him, but with poor, wrinkly, greasy Joe and his crappy mindset, it's no use that the woman he's been crushing on creepily for eight months has finally figured out that he's alive. She couldn't possibly be interested in me. Why would she ask me out? I don't even have enough money to buy myself dinner, let alone her too… He politely tells her that he has something important to do this evening and he walks away quickly before she can respond. He feels embarrassed that he lied to her. I hope I can turn things around soon, and then I could ask her–No! I'm just a dirty, lazy piece of shit. I have nothing to offer her. I don't want to waste her time—as much as I'd like to.

Joe used to have friends, but he always came up with reasons why it was an inconvenient day or time for whatever they had planned. Eventually, they stopped asking altogether. *What is wrong with me?* He often wonders what he could have done differently. He thinks of the past and questions the decisions he's made...over...and over...and over...and over...

PART 1:

This Is
The First Part

CHAPTER 1:

THE SCIENCE OF SYNAPSES

You've probably heard somewhere at one time or another that complaining literally rewires your brain. You probably also rolled your eyes at yet another piece of scientific information that's probably not true. Except, it is.

Whenever you have a thought, a neuron in your brain will send a signal to another neuron, essentially forming a bridge for the signal to cross, also known as a synapse. Even your brain is naturally lazy, as the more a thought is triggered in the brain, the closer the synapses grow together to make it easier for the electrical charge of that thought to travel across that "bridge." The brain is physically restructuring itself to make it easier for your most frequent thoughts to process in your brain.

Therefore, when you are chronically negative, you are essentially making it easier for your brain to have negative thoughts. When it comes time for you to form a thought, the one that has the shortest distance to travel is the one that will be prominent in your brain.

So there you have it. Thinking positively isn't just something that can force a smile on your face on a stressful day. It can actually literally rewire you into having a less stressful, more enjoyable, and positive existence every day. Without fully comprehending the background behind why positive thinking actually works, many believe it's just a bunch of hippie, mumbo jumbo, jibber jabber preached by overly happy people who seem to have it all together. The truth is, there is legitimate science that backs up their happiness and positivity, so these people you may scoff at are actually on to something.

So, let's say that you are on your way to work and you happen to have a very hard-to-handle boss that you do not like very much. (This is of course very rare, so you may not be able to relate.) Each day that you go to work, something irritable arises that reminds you how much you dislike them and you realize that the relationship between you two will likely never change, thus making work itself stressful and challenging for you to enjoy.

This particular situation would create a series of memories that result in work being classified as painful to you. These memories would all build upon each other, creating great stress around work itself, even though the problem is actually not with your work, but with your boss. Now, each time you prepare to leave for work, your morning routine triggers synapses within your brain, which results in memories of the stress being brought to the forefront. As a result, your biology literally begins to generate its own stress as a way to attempt to protect you from the stress that you are about to encounter at work. Work becomes your trigger and stress becomes your response.

This will continue growing and building as the memories of stress at your work grow larger and larger. Now, every time you go to work, the stress response becomes bigger each time until it is so large that you can no longer handle it. You may begin to carry this stress with you everywhere, finding all sorts of different negative symptoms of it within your life. Maybe you are not sleeping as soundly through the night. Maybe you are struggling to keep up a healthy appetite. Maybe you are craving more unhealthy comfort foods than normal. Maybe all of the areas of your life are impacted as your relationships, self-care, health, and emotions all deteriorate in the face of this overwhelming stress. Before you know it, all of your thoughts grow to be negative, not just those surrounding work.

Anything that triggers you to remember work or any of the new stresses you have introduced into your life, because of this stress bubbling over, results in more and more stress. (Have I said the word stress enough yet?) For example, perhaps because you were so upset from work one day, that when you went to the grocery store right after work, it seemed unbearable because you were miserable already. The lines were too long, you couldn't find anything you needed (why did they move the peanut butter to a different aisle??), and you kept dropping things or otherwise just having difficulty with the entire experience.

Now, your brain begins to build associations and memories of simple tasks such as grocery shopping as being stressful. And now you hate lines of people and peanut butter. And what did the peanut butter ever do to you?? So, the cycle continues and the stress permeates throughout your entire life until before you know it, all areas of your life have left you feeling stressed, overwhelmed, and buried under the weight of it all.

As you can see, synapses are powerful and this negativity cycle can happen quickly, spiraling you out of control before you even know what happened. A biological response that is meant to support and protect you, in the end, is doing more damage and creating more troubles for you to deal with. Congratulations, you now have a ~~bitch inside your head~~ mean inner voice and you can't seem to help but fall into its grasp, becoming more bitter and judgmental every day. This is the point where you see random people smiling and want to stick needles in their eyes. When all this science-y stuff is not working in our favor, it can truly make things go from bad to worse because our perception of our surroundings and circumstances, and how we react to them grow more and more negative.

Fortunately for you, if synapses have the capacity to destroy your good vibes, they also have the capacity to heal them. You can actually undo the negative wiring and rewire your brain to become more positive, healthy, and joyful overall. Given that negativity-wiring requires persistent worrying and negative thoughts, it makes sense that rewiring your brain for positivity requires you to have persistent positive thoughts. (Go ahead, tell your brain good vibes only, please.) In essence, intentionally thinking of positive things repeatedly will make science happen in your brain, then just as negativity from one aspect of your life spilled over into other aspects and created a plethora of negativity, your positivity will also do the same. Your positive thinking will begin to grow, and it will send a flood of positivity into other areas of your life.

Although it may be hard to believe it now since you have not yet been intentionally training your brain's synapses, your negativity can actually be rewritten using this method. Soon, your grocery shopping trips will be enjoyable, you will find joy in the traffic on your way home from work, and you will begin searching for ways to enjoy your job despite your difficult boss. The many areas of your life that have been encumbered by negativity (including peanut butter) will go on to be rewritten and be replaced with positivity and enhanced by happy thoughts.

However, it is important to understand that this will be an ongoing process that takes time. If you consider how many years you have been ~~bitching~~ complaining, worrying, and listening to your inner mean girl, you can conclude that it has likely taken a long time for you to get to where you are now. Even if you only recall things really becoming bad recently, it was probably unknowingly building up for quite some time. Therefore, it won't be an overnight task to get out of the dark side and step into the light.

Recognizing how and why your brain automatically jumps to negative emotions like stress, pessimism, worry, and fear will support you in understanding that in most instances, your troubles are not caused by your circumstances but rather by your brain and the way it functions. Then, you can shut that negative voice the hell up and welcome your inner hippie Pollyanna to help you experience a greater life. This does not necessarily mean that negativity will never arise. Instead, it simply means that you will be able to cope through difficulties better when it does, and you will develop a far more optimistic outlook on life and the world around overall.

REESE OWEN

CHAPTER 2:

STRESS—IT'S WHAT'S FOR DINNER

Stress is a regular fact of life. Everyone experiences it on a daily basis and virtually everyone experiences troublesome bouts of stress that seem to last several days, weeks, months, or even years at a time. Considering the way our modern society is built, stress is often experienced in unnaturally high levels. It is the result of our disconnectedness, our sense of obligation to everything and everyone else, and our inability to understand our own needs and how we can best take care of ourselves. Still, just because we tend to experience stress in unhealthy levels does not mean that stress itself is a bad thing.

Experiencing stress is actually a natural biological occurrence that happens with a very constructive purpose. When we are not experiencing chronic levels of heightened stress, we have the opportunity to use stress as a natural support in our lives. Healthy levels of stress actually promote our desire to do better in life, thus encouraging us to reach peak levels and work successfully towards our goals and desires. Understanding how to identify and manage stress, and use it in a helpful and productive way is key for mental health. By keeping your stress levels healthy, your body functions normally, and you can reap the benefits that stress can offer you.

Under situations where stress begins to build up within you, your body's adrenal glands will secrete a hormone called cortisol. Cortisol pushes you into a fight or flight response. This, when used properly, can be extremely supportive in your life.

Let's say you are sitting on your couch one day and you realize that you are unhappy with your life as it is. You feel that your job is not challenging you, you are not making enough money, you dislike the home you are living in, and you wish you had more discretionary funds to do the things that you enjoy. When you recall your life experiences, you realize that you are tremendously unhappy with the way things are and you wish that they were better. So, you begin to feel stressed out.

In response, science happens. Your body begins to secrete that cortisol because you are realizing how uncomfortable you are with your life. So, as this cortisol begins to build up, you find yourself feeling a tremendous amount of energy within you that is preparing you to do something--Fight or flight. Do or die. Now or never. Sink or swim. Get rich or die trying. Okay, you get the point. You begin to feel within you all the energy you need to either run and hide from your problems or to face them and actually do something about them.

This means that you now have the motivation within you to make changes and pursue a life you would actually enjoy. Instead of sitting around feeling like a wrinkly, greasy loser, you now have what it takes to feel truly capable of making changes, get a better job with better pay, and find yourself somewhere to live that doesn't make you feel like you're in a Property Brothers "before" house. When experienced productively so to speak, cortisol and stress can actually become exhilarating feelings.

For many, the exclusion of stress means that they actually struggle to find motivation to do anything that they desire to do. When they are unhappy with things, rather than having the adrenaline present to push them to make changes, they simply become complacent and depressed. This is another type of stress per se, but it is one that will not actually push them to do anything positive. Instead, the individual will sit and find themselves moving into unhealthy stress levels that can begin to damage their well-being.

The key here is being able to identify the stress, and then having the self-esteem to meet it and realize that you are capable of making changes. Upon combining your drive with the energy granted to you by stress, you can create a powerful concoction that leads you to create and achieve massive, wonderful things in your life.

This very chemical reaction is why some people actually work better under stress. People who find themselves working harder with greater motivation, focus, and determination closer to their deadlines are unknowingly using the stress as a means to support their capacity to achieve their goals. Athletes who thrive in highly competitive situations are also using these stress chemicals to support them in achieving success in their desired hobbies or careers. Likewise, highly stressed career-oriented people have a tendency to be driven by the stress and thus they produce greater results. Where some crack under pressure, some use that pressure to their advantage.

Rather than falling victim to the inner mean voice, you need to silence it and trust that you have what it takes to generate success in your life. This is where you can use your synapses to your advantage—yay science! Remember—you can literally rewire your brain to have the capacity to trust and believe in yourself. (More on that later.) Then, you can pistol whip your inner mean girl, take back your mental positivity, and begin acting in a way that allows you to use the stress to your advantage.

The problem, then, is not in the existence of stress and cortisol themselves. Instead, the problem lies in people not knowing how to successfully manage, use, and release this state in a healthy way that prevents it from building up and becoming stuck within the body, therefore causing people to be mentally "stuck" within their minds. In order to learn how to use stress successfully in a positive way, people first need to de-stress as completely as possible. Stress that has not been "used" and is no longer serving the purpose of initiating present and immediate action has likely built up over time and thus become destructive.

If you first experienced stress six weeks ago when you were supposed to start that project, and you didn't, that stress didn't prompt you to immediate action in that moment, so now the stress you've been holding on to from the task left undone is becoming destructive rather than constructive, and resulting in excess cortisol in your body. This can cause many negative mental reactions including anxiety, depression, inability to control emotions, and irritability just to name a few.

It can also cause adverse physical symptoms in the body including high blood pressure, headaches, fatigue. All around bad news. We want to lower cortisol levels and eliminate bad stress so you can ensure that you start from a clean slate.

Using stress to your advantage can play a major role in helping you remain healthy. This does not mean that stress won't be…well, stressful. But, it does mean that you will begin to gain the benefits of stress rather than suffer with the negative side effects that it can bring. Once upon a time, stress was a biological factor we used in order to run away from predators and capture prey. It was essential to our very survival in such a way that it truly was solely responsible for our ability to stay alive. It drove our instincts and gave us the energy needed to accomplish whatever we needed to do to survive in the caveman days.

But when's the last time you saw a caveman? (Your awful date from Tinder that looked nothing like their picture doesn't count.) Although we no longer live in such a savage world (although at times it can feel like it), stress still exists, and it still has the same purpose within us. Learning to apply it to your life in a way that puts it to good productive use will support you in making sure that you do not experience unhealthy stress, and it will aid you in having greater success in all that you do.

.

CHAPTER 3:

THE SURVIVAL INSTINCT THAT'S KILLING YOU FROM THE INSIDE OUT

Believe it or not, negativity is actually (as the chapter title suggests) a survival instinct. (But that's not the end of the story, so don't go rubbing this in the face of your most obnoxiously happy friend.) Only since the modernization of democracy and law did "innocent until proven guilty" become an actual thing. Before that, we were all about "guilty until proven innocent." Why do I bring up law stuff in a book of science-y stuff? Because it helps explain why in being overly cautious, we could actually survive. If people seemed creepy or dangerous, well, better safe than sorry, let's just lock them up and assume that they are. This is not a method of executing justice that I'm suggesting we stick to nowadays, but it used to work back in the day…kind of…not really.

If we go even further back to pre-civilization, back in those caveman days, those who were naïve or who did not think to stay hyperaware of their surroundings would surely be hunted and thus they would die. Of course, life is not nearly as dangerous anymore. We're not cavemen, after all, and we do not have to fear being plucked out of a tree by a saber-toothed tiger.

While we still have freak accidents that cause death and we have not (yet) found a way to be invincible and live forever, our lives are much simpler and require a lot less alertness and preparedness than they once did. Without the worry that a predator will find us and eat us, we can sit and relax a little and enjoy the general comfort and safety of our homes. There is no more need to fight for our survival in that way anymore.

Yet still, from a young age, we naturally lean toward negativity and are wired to believe the negative. Naturally, this means that our synapses get a good head start on instilling those negative thoughts in our heads. So by the time we become adults, and "life" hits, this means that we have to work that much more intentionally to get those synapses working in our favor so that we can become more positive. Additionally, it means that we are literally just doing what our bodies told us to do in order to survive our circumstances even when they are not deadly.

According to many people in white lab coats and glasses (also known as scientists), our natural tendency to lean toward negativity and to live as pessimists actually drove human evolution at one point. The negativity bias that we all live with, which is the biological tendency to be an Eeyore and see everything with a dark light, means that we grant ourselves the ability to ensure that we are never ill-prepared for danger because we are always expecting it. So, according to your brain, by always believing that your boss is going to be a jerk, you prepare yourself for when they actually are one.

Or by assuming your relationship won't work out, or the business deal won't go through, or that your offer won't be accepted on the house you want, you are not caught by surprise when things don't go your way and the pain caused by that disappointment is not as damaging.

Essentially, negativity bias is in action any time you naturally respond with judgment, bitterness, mistrust, or other negativity without really having any concrete or logical reason why. For example, if you have always passed tests with flying colors and you are extremely confident in the material you are being tested on, yet you feel an intense fear of failure following the test, this is your negativity bias. Logically, you know there is no way that you will fail the test. However, your brain will tell you that you have to prepare yourself mentally for the disappointment that you would experience if you did, thus lessening the blow and the pain you would experience under that circumstance.

Although it can have some positive benefits, negativity bias unfortunately infiltrates many areas of our lives. We have a tendency to constantly believe that we are in danger or at risk and therefore, we actually heighten our stress hormones and cause ourselves to feel the unhealthy effects of chronic stress that we often feel victimized by.

Low self-esteem and low self-confidence make matters even worse, causing us to feel held hostage by the negative thoughts and expectations, because we feel that we cannot overcome them. We start to believe the limiting thoughts that are planted in our minds due to our negativity bias. Because of this, we don't take action and don't see any positive change in our lives, so the low self-esteem and low self-confidence get worse and the cycle continues.

Despite being responsible for our evolution as a species and the few other positive benefits we gain from negativity bias, it is not something we need to live with in our modern-day lives. It now causes more harm than good and has become a negative trait more than it is a positive trait. We have evolved enough that we no longer require it in such a high degree.

Understanding negativity bias and all that it brings means two really great things for most people. The first thing is that it's not your fault. Isn't that great? You can release accountability and blame it on nature. Nothing is more comforting to a person whose life isn't going the way they want than a good old-fashioned scapegoat. Your natural tendency toward negativity is actually biological and chances are you are not intentionally pessimistic, rather you are naturally pessimistic.

The second thing is that we have reached a point in our evolution where we are not constantly pessimistic, meaning we can actually overcome negativity bias and eliminate it from our psyche. This does not mean that you will never experience it again, particularly if you do not remain in practice with your positive thinking, but it does mean that you can get a handle on it and reduce or eliminate its negative impact altogether depending on your dedication to doing so.

In the earlier example of the test, you could use logic and rationale to rewire your brain regarding this specific concern. You can undo that negativity bias by affirming to yourself that you are confident in the material and you know there is no way that you would fail because you studied hard, and you are a frickin genius in this subject. By telling yourself repeatedly that you're a frickin genius, you begin to restructure your brain, creating shorter distances for the positive thoughts to be transmitted from neuron to neuron. You're making it easier and easier for you to think positive. The more you do this, the more it will work and the less it will be a challenge for you to overcome your natural negativity bias in the future. It's a classic case of the more you do something, the easier it becomes. This works for both positive and negative thinking, so use this power consciously and wisely.

Even though the negative voice is biological and natural and has likely been with you since birth, it's time for it to take a hike. Better yet, take a hike and get eaten by a bear. Replace the Negative Nancy in your head with positive affirmations and you'll be surprised at how much confidence you gain.

Many psychologists refer to negativity bias as mental laziness because it is a default setting. You hear that? Automatically going to the negative is lazy. Just because it is the default setting for you, however, does not mean that it needs to stay that way. You don't leave your smartphone on the default settings. You change that wallpaper, change that ringtone, and customize those home screen icons as soon as you get your phone. So go ahead, customize your features, kick that negative voice the hell out, and start celebrating yourself. Recognize when negativity bias comes in and if all else fails, yell "NO!" in its little punk face. (But maybe don't do that in public.) Start sweet talking yourself to remind yourself that you are awesome and of course good things will happen for you. (Maybe also don't do that in public either.)

And remember, if things don't go as planned, do not fret because it is not the end of the world. Most things can be fixed or redone. You can always retake the test, apologize for being late, or remember your anniversary next year. There is no reason to think that any negative experience is "total doom" like that incessant voice likes to have you believe.

As you continue rewriting your negative gut-kick reactions with positive affirmations and thus budding self-confidence, you will teach your brain to realize that there is no need to automatically respond to situations with negativity. Who says you can't teach an old dog new tricks? Again, this does not mean that you will never experience negativity, nor does it mean that you will never have initial out-of-the-blue negative reactions to your environment, circumstances, or experiences. But once you develop that positivity muscle, you will be able to quickly flex those happy mental biceps, debunk those Eeyore thoughts, and move into a positive train of thought that promotes happiness, joy, and reduced stress in your life.

CHAPTER 4:

DRIVING YOURSELF INSANE

Have you ever experienced a situation where you were so pessimistic that you actually made yourself feel insane? You had no reason to believe in any of the pessimistic thoughts swirling through your brain and yet you felt incapable of changing your mind, and so it felt like you were hopeless in the face of it all?

This is not an uncommon experience. At least once in their lifetime, a person will feel so negative and untrusting or miserable that they make themselves feel literally crazy. They likely know that there is no genuine reason for them to feel this way and yet, for the life of them, they cannot seem to stop. This happens for two reasons: our good old friends negativity bias and synapses. Yes, once again they come into play.

When you are biologically wired to be a pessimist and your brain has all of the perfect neural pathways to support pessimism, being any different is a challenge. Furthermore, if you have no idea why this is happening, it can be easy to think that there is something wrong with you and wonder why you can't just "think positively already, dammit!" I mean, that's what they tell you to do, isn't it? In many cases, when you are feeling down or negative about something, people say "think positive!" in a nonchalant or annoyingly cheery voice. It is as though they actually believe this lame, pathetic advice will actually work.

Only, it will. But what those annoyingly happy people don't tell you is that it takes time, practice, and intention to get there. People have a way of making positivity sound so easy, yet it is not always so— especially when you have not yet come to understand how and why negativity and positivity work in the brain and what you can actually do about it. Thus, this can be one of the most challenging, insulting, and dangerous pieces of advice given when it is not accompanied by genuine advice on how to think positively.

See, after you have driven yourself crazy with negativity and then you are told to "just think positive," a common next step is to move into Phase Two of the crazy (yes, there are phases to this thing): obsession and self-doubt. You begin to obsess over how to think positively, and you look for people who are already doing it. In many cases, these successfully positive people are not recounting how challenging it once was because they've already made it to the other side, so it's easy for them to see everything with a rainbow sparkle filter. As a result, you read their books or free handouts and you listen to them religiously and yet for some reason, you cannot seem to reach their level of positivity. Now, you're driving yourself crazy all over again. Only this time it is not because of the negativity itself but because you feel entrapped by it.

When you watch people who are already successfully thinking positively and living in that positive frame of mind, it can be easy to compare yourself against them and wonder why you are so negative. What's wrong with me? Why can't I just think like that? Why can't I just see things the way they see them? Then, you begin to hop deeper into the negativity passage. And let me tell you, it is a deep and seemingly never-ending passage. You start judging yourself harshly for not being happy enough, you roll your eyes when you see their social media posts and feel like their advice is not working, and you get grumpier and grumpier wondering why you cannot seem to kick this terrible pessimistic voice that will not seem to just shut the hell up already.

This is because you are trying to reach level 100 without doing levels 1-99 first. What video game lets you go straight to the end right after starting it? What movie has only an opening and an ending scene? One thing many people fail to realize when they embark on their journey to positivity is that it can actually be a slow and lingering process. Kind of like that crappy movie your significant other always tries to force you to watch. But even when you are dedicated to your positivity cause day in and day out, it takes time to go from Eeyore to Tigger. Add into that the self-doubt and self-hatred you feel when you have not reached level 100 instantaneously, and you will find yourself yet again holding yourself back from experiencing positivity.

Once you've embarked on your positive affirmations journey, you can't simultaneously listen to your subconscious mean voice. In other words, your conscious positive voice is being echoed and overshadowed by that brat in the background who is not yet willing to give up. You are still being overruled by your negativity bias. Don't let it win. It's trying to save you from the hurt of not succeeding, but ironically, in doing so, it directly becomes the primary reason why you are not succeeding.

Driving yourself crazy with misery and negativity and then driving yourself crazy with trying to overcome them are two very common states that virtually everyone experiences on their path to becoming a more positive person. It is important to understand that these are two natural states and that you will overcome them if you stay dedicated. Giving yourself the chance to recognize these backdoor opportunities for negativity bias to resurface is important.

With this, you give yourself the capacity to understand why you are not actually experiencing any success with your attempts at positivity. Then, you can begin unwinding the secretive negativity bias from your life and move on to feeling far more confident and successful with your positivity exercises. You are doing your positivity exercises, aren't you? Remember those affirmations—I am a badass. I am a badass. I am a badass…But doing this might actually backfire if each time you say, "I am a badass!" your subconscious says, "No, you are actually a pansy!" That would actually be wiring your brain further for negativity and pessimism.

The easiest way to stop driving yourself crazy in this way is to just stop. Of course, that's also the hardest way. When you realize that you are bullying yourself for not being "good enough," "positive enough," "successful enough," or any other type of "enough," just stop. Aren't you tired of that? If that negative voice was personified by an actual human being outside of you, you would stop hanging out with them, block them, and ghost them out of your life. It's time to ghost the inner mean girl, douchebag, whatever you want to call the otherwise unhelpful, unsupportive, negative voice inside your head.

Confront that rude voice that will not leave you alone and ask it why on earth it is speaking. Keeping a journal handy for this practice is incredibly important. Then, you can sit down, confront the voice, and begin writing out the dialogue that takes place between you. This gets the situation out of the intangible inside your head and into the tangible on the paper in front of you. That way you can begin understanding that the logic behind the mean voice is fractured and, in many cases, nonexistent. Instead, it is simply speaking out of its natural tendency. Nothing to take personally. When you realize this, it becomes a lot easier to actually deny it any power within your mind, stand firm, and be confident because you now know with logic, reason, and evidence that this voice is untrue and is not serving you.

Only after you have confronted, debunked, and ruled out the messages of your inner mean voice can you begin reaping benefits of your positivity practices. That way, as you are repeating your positive affirmations, you are actually re-wiring your brain for positivity, rather than counteracting your efforts by further reinforcing the negativity within it.

CHAPTER 5:

REMOVING TOXICITY

Removing toxicity from your life takes time, care, patience, and consistent effort. For many of us, our everyday lives expose us to a great deal of stress and toxicity. Toxicity arises in many key areas of our lives, most notably including work and relationships.

When it comes to work, toxicity often arises when you have negative relationships with coworkers or your boss, when you feel underappreciated, or when your work environment is toxic in and of itself. This becomes particularly challenging for many people because work is a necessity in order for us to make a living and live a good life. The whole "working thing" is kind of a requirement if you're not into things like, you know poverty and struggle.

Removing toxicity from your work can be tackled a few different ways. If you are lucky, you may be able to quit your job and get a new one working somewhere that is far more supportive and healthier for you. Or, you may have a special talent or passion that allows you to choose entrepreneurship, which in turns lets you become your own boss.

If you are not able to take radical action to make one of the aforementioned changes, you still need to consider what action you can take. Perhaps you can bring the toxicity to the attention of your boss or human resources, turn your attention and focus to things that are more positive about your job, and learn how to properly advocate for yourself and set boundaries with people who are detrimental to your climb to Pollyanna baddassery. Knowing how to stand up to people and how to say no to toxic situations can be a great place to start if you are looking to improve your work life conditions without taking radical action such as quitting or starting your own business.

Relationships are another area that pose great challenges because, as humans, we crave connection in our lives. We want to be close and connected with the people around us because this supports us in feeling loved and accepted. When we lack closeness with others, we fail to thrive as humans, as this has a very negative impact on our psyche. As such, we sometimes find ourselves accepting less-than-acceptable situations within our relationships because we fear not getting or losing love and acceptance. This can be especially tricky when we've already established a relationship with a toxic person, and thus have a hard time risking the loss of someone we care about and who we see as a part of our "tribe."

Removing toxicity from your relationships takes effort and patience. In many cases, it will require you to sever relationships, as difficult as this may be. I know. It will be hard. But it will be worth it for your own mental and emotional health. You can't expect to not be an Eeyore anymore if you're still surrounding yourself with Eeyores. Seeking support and assistance in getting through the phase of leaving a toxic relationship may be required depending on who the relationship was with. In other cases, you may simply be able to minimize the time that you spend with said person.

That being said, not all relationships will require you to sever them or reduce the time you spend with the person. Although, this next tactic is not any easier for the same reason that it's easier to ghost a person than actually break up with them. This tactic will require discomfort and having difficult conversations. In some cases, you may be able to resolve the toxicity by bringing it to the awareness of the individual and sharing with them how their behavior affects you.

By sharing openly and honestly with the other person, you give yourself the opportunity to maintain the good part of the relationship, but lose the part that makes it insufferable for you. Be honest with them. Tell them you don't like it when they always have a snide remark, or always say something negative about how you look, or always put down your goals and plans.

If the other person accepts and you begin focusing on improving your relationship, then you get to celebrate that your relationship has been saved, and that you pushed yourself through a process that most people are so uncomfortable doing that they'd rather fake their own death. If your openness backfires, however, it may be time to release that person and trust in yourself enough to make new friends or find a new lover. If they are family, it may be more of a challenge, but it might be the necessary action that you have to take to honor yourself and preserve your well-being.

Now that we've spent all that time talking about other people, it's time to point the finger back in the mirror again. (I know, I know, this isn't the fun part. It's more fun when it's everyone else's fault.) Aside from the evil voice in our heads and our natural tendency towards negativity bias, there are other ways that we can become toxic to ourselves. When we fail to recognize our needs, advocate for ourselves, prioritize self-development and self-mastery, or achieve personal growth, we fail ourselves. We begin to practice things like self-neglect and self-abandonment that can lead to us becoming our own personal nightmare. This is extremely common and can be hard to face. However, if you want to remove toxicity from your life, you will need to openly and honestly accept yourself for who you are and be willing to admit to this and most importantly work toward improving it.

If you have become toxic towards yourself, you will know it. It is obvious in the way that you treat yourself and in the way that you feel about yourself. Becoming toxic to yourself looks like not caring about yourself, not trusting yourself, not feeling confident about yourself, or not respecting yourself. If you're really effing up, it may look like all of those things combined. You may deny yourself the right to pleasure and joy believing that you are not worthy, force yourself into doing more than you can reasonably handle because you feel that it is your duty to care for others and not yourself, or bully yourself to the point of not being able to perform various tasks and duties because you are being so harsh on yourself.

Getting to this point is not uncommon, especially with a person who has not yet had the opportunity to begin consciously making an effort towards controlling their mind. You may see other people feeling happy, confident, joyful, and seemingly carefree while you yourself feel the wrath of your own self-neglect, self-abandonment and self-hatred. If this is the case, know that you are in the wrong place, that there is nothing wrong with you, and that you can overcome this.

Removing the toxicity that you express toward yourself in your own life takes more time and attention because, naturally, you cannot remove yourself from your own life. So, instead, you need to focus on learning how to love yourself once again. Then, you can actually understand yourself and your needs and develop a personal relationship (with yourself) that supports you in having greater success in your life. When you begin to head down this positive new path, you will find it much easier to love yourself, care for yourself, and listen to your inner nice voice. Trust that you have what it takes to make a difference in your own life and that you can and will have a positive impact on your own existence.

CHAPTER 6:

THREE DAILY HABITS YOU NEED TO START PRACTICING TODAY (OH, AND EVERY DAY AFTER THAT)

Okay, here's another part that people don't always like—work. Yes, you have to actually do something to make changes and get results. If you recall from the previous chapters, some practices were given to you to start incorporating into your life, but now, I'm going to add some more things to your plate and perhaps reframe some of what has already been mentioned in little, short, actionable tasks. Lucky for you, there are only three. We are going to cover three daily habits that you need to start practicing today so that you can set a strong foundation for silencing that negative voice and moving toward a positive and more wholesome and happy life. That's three daily habits. That means you have to do them every day. Not every other day, you don't get the weekends off—every day. The whole habit thing doesn't really work unless you do it every time.

Now that you understand how and why negativity exists in your life, it is time for you to begin taking some consistent action in destroying it so that you can go on to conquer a life you love and deserve. Here is what you need to do each day:

Habit #1: Confront Yourself

The first thing that you need to do is confront yourself. The reality is that this inner voice is probably keeping you from your own best life more than you even realize it. These voices have a tendency to be sneaky and, in many cases, we do not realize it until it feels like we're past the point of no return.

At the first sign of any negative thought, I want you to stop completely. Such negative thoughts can include things like "I look fat in this," "That person would never find me attractive," "I'm not good enough to get that promotion," "I'm not good enough," "My idea is stupid," or "I'll never finish the project in time."

Whether you are going about daily life or if you are in the middle of your positivity practice, as soon as a negative though pops up, you need to stop and begin confronting this voice. Take a couple minutes to dive into your journal and unpack the internal dialogue. Make a conscious effort to understand what the voice is saying, why it is saying it, and what it is attempting to protect you from.

Then, debunk it. Bring evidence, logic, and rationality into play to encourage yourself to recognize the voice as false. If you don't have a journal or notebook around, use your phone to take down the notes. If you don't have a phone, take mental notes. After you have confronted yourself, change the voice and affirm your new belief.

So, if the voice said "You will never get that raise because you are not worthy," you may discover that it may be telling you that because it doesn't want you to be embarrassed if your petition to get a raise doesn't go over well with your boss. It may be trying to protect you from the disappointment you'd feel if you'd already made plans for what you'd buy if you got that raise but didn't end up getting the raise. But you can counteract that by telling yourself that you are the most qualified and hardest working person in your department, based on your performance reviews your boss loves you, and you've already been told how much value you add to the company. You are more than worthy, and of course you're getting a raise!

Habit #2: Cheer For Yourself

The next practice you need to start doing on a daily basis is celebrating yourself and being your biggest cheerleader. This does not need to come after a bout of negativity or confronting your inner voice. Instead, it can and should be practiced all on its own. When you wake up in the morning, list off three positive things you anticipate experiencing that day and celebrate them in advance. Then, at the end of the day, find three things that actually happened and celebrate those. So this habit is two-fold. You're creating opportunities to expect and manifest positive outcomes in your life, and also identifying areas where you can pat yourself on the back for a job well done. The more you do this, the better you will feel.

This begins laying the ground work for you to have a more positive outlook in general because you are now approaching your life and reflecting on your life with optimism rather than pessimism. As a result, guess what those synapses are doing? That's right—rewiring your brain and supporting you in becoming a true optimist!

Habit #3: Reframe One Big Thing

Negative bias often works on memories to provide evidence as to why it is "right." Learning to reframe your daily events so that you see them through optimism can adjust how you store memories and thus, result in your negative bias having less evidence to draw on. This is a great way to silence your negative inner voice while also building your repertoire of positive evidence that supports you in having greater belief in yourself, self-confidence, and self-esteem.

Each day, you should recall your daily events and choose at least one stressful occurrence and reframe it. For example, say you were late to work because of a traffic incident and got yelled at by your boss for being late. Instead of seeing this as a memory that allows you to recall why your boss is so mean, you can use this as a memory to recall why you are so lucky that you made it safely to work and that you were not a part of the traffic incident.

Reframing your memories in a more positive light will not only help you in the long term, but it also helps to immediately reduce any stress you are feeling in the short term. Stress like that can linger and carry residual stress into your sleep so that even when you are unconscious, you are still not free from your brain's negative strongholds. This residual stress can compound and build even faster. Reducing it by reframing before you fall asleep will ensure that you go to sleep with a peaceful mind, thus giving you a peaceful sleep and a clean slate to start on tomorrow.

Like what you see so far?

Please leave a review on Amazon
letting us know!

PART 2:

This Is
The Second Part

CHAPTER 7:

HOW YOUR BRAIN TELLS YOU TO FREAK OUT

Let's talk a little neurobiology. Yay, more science! When you experience fear and worry, what is ultimately happening is that the part of your brain responsible for thinking provides feedback to the part of your brain that is responsible for producing emotions. This is how you determine whether you are safe or unsafe in your surroundings. Using this same communication pattern, you can quickly be driven into a heightened state which can turn into either fear (bad) or excitement (good).

If this communication translates into fear, this begins the worrying process in your body. When you worry, the amygdala, which is a part of your brain, is essentially letting your brain know that the sensory signals that it is interpreting are alerting for danger. This part of your brain is responsible for letting the rest of your brain know that it can either relax or that it needs to begin producing other necessary responses to protect you from the danger it is perceiving. Emotional memories that we experience within our lifetimes are stored directly in the center of the amygdala which supports it in being able to determine situations that are risky. Anything that produced emotional trauma or danger in the past would be perceived as capable of producing it again in the present or future. This causes the rest of the brain to begin responding in a way that produces the hormones required to jump-start your body into action and get you ready to either fight or flight.

And let's not forget the role that the hippocampus plays in all of this. The hippocampus is specifically responsible for remembering threatening events and storing them as memories so that you can prevent yourself from reliving these experiences in the real world. You can thank your hippocampus for being the reason you don't go around sticking your head in the oven every day. If you touched a hot stove when you were a child and burned yourself, your hippocampus recognizes this danger, turns it into a memory, and informs your brain that any time this danger is perceived to be risky in the future, the body must act in a certain way to prevent it.

The hippocampus tends to be smaller in individuals who experience some form of serious trauma in their lives. For example, people who were victims of abuse (especially in childhood) and people who served in combat in the military tend to have a smaller hippocampus. The reduction in size of this part of the brain results in these particular individuals experiencing fragmented memories, particularly surrounding the trauma, which leads to flashbacks to traumatic events. For that reason, individuals who have suffered with notable trauma in their lives are known to be at higher risk of experiencing mental distress and worry than others.

As with many things, there is a positive and a negative side. Anxiety and worry have a powerful ability to fuel the body and protect you from dangerous situations. When the body is operating healthfully, these two emotions operate nearly the same as stress does. The primary difference, however, is that stress is typically just felt as an overwhelming physical feeling within the body, whereas anxiety and worry can present mental distress through thoughts and feelings.

So, say you come home after a hard day at work and you are feeling stressed out. You may be a little overwhelmed and uncomfortable, but you are not likely to have any one particular thought entrapped in your mind. Alternatively, if you are experiencing anxiety or worry, it is likely that you are extremely focused on the world around you and that you may be hypersensitive to various things or obsessing over one particular thing. This will depend on whether you are experiencing anxiety or worry towards one specific situation or in general.

Having bouts of anxiety and worry is still normal, even when they become seemingly out of control. Even perfectly healthy adults can experience panic attacks without having to be diagnosed with any form of mental or emotional disorder or condition that would trigger the attack. These are simply chemical responses to life that happen within the brain and occasionally get beyond our control.

However, having frequent or unstoppable bouts of anxiety and worry on an ongoing basis can signal that something is wrong. While some people may genuinely need medication and professional support in finding solace from these symptoms, others may find that through mental training and strengthening, they are able to find freedom from their symptoms so that they can go on to have a healthy psyche once more.

If you find that you are having frequent bouts of anxiety or worry or that you feel like you are freaking out to an extent that it is causing severe disruption and discomfort in your life, it is time that you start taking better care of your mental health. There are many things that you can do to strengthen your mental health, which will not only support you in eliminating worry and anxiety, but will also support you in experiencing greater positivity in your mind. When you put in the work to eliminate problematic anxiety and stress, you are actually using tools that are powerful in helping you silence your inner voice so that you can get back to those good vibes only. Through this, you can free yourself of the limitations bestowed upon you by the toxic voice in your head that loves to bring you down.

So what's the best way to eliminate worry? Be prepared to be shocked. I'm about to rock your world. We're about to go where no man has gone before. Not really. You probably won't be surprised to learn that one of the best things you can do to eradicate worry and silence your negative inner voice is meditation.

Meditation is highly praised for—let's be honest, pretty much everything. It's pretty high up there right along with coconut oil, apple cider vinegar, and a Beyonce album for being a fix-all solution. Using meditation as a way to regain control over your mind may be something you've heard before, but have you done it? Have you done it consistently? If you haven't, then let's be real—you needed to hear again about how something that ironically entails doing pretty much nothing can fix pretty much everything.

Meditating does not have to be some long, drawn-out ritual of candles and gongs and incense and elephant print pants and contorted cirque du soleil body positions that takes hours out of your daily life. You don't have to sell all your belongings, grow your hair to your waist, and live off the land to meditate. Although, you can certainly be that person if that is who you desire to become. Hey, I'm not judging. But in all seriousness, meditation is an incredible tool to use so that you can begin training that brain of yours and releasing its chronic need to freak out.

A great little practice that you can incorporate to get started is to meditate for just ten minutes, and then follow it by your favorite music. Studies show that incorporating even just ten minutes of meditation into your daily routine is optimal for supporting your brain in learning to relax. Giving it the time to learn how to tune out the outer world and just experience peace is crucial to your mental health. And the good news is that mediation is one of the easiest things you could ever do. All you do is sit down, close your eyes, clear your mind, and do nothing. This is where those synapses come into play again, creating new neural pathways that remind your brain that it is okay to calm down and relax every so often! Following it by good music is wonderful, too.

Now, I wouldn't recommend following up your meditation session with Nirvana, Smells Like Teen

Spirit or anything like that, but music has a way of "bringing you back to reality" from your meditation practice, and it has a wonderful healing effect on our brains. Listening to some of your favorite music and getting up to move around afterwards can help stimulate joy and positivity in your mind. If you love dancing, you can dance. If you don't fancy yourself a dancer, just moving around and doing some chores around your house or even working out is great too. The idea is that you want to use the music as a tool to move the excess energy through you so that you can get back to feeling good again.

There are also many other personal rituals that you can create that can support you in putting a pause on your freak outs. Finding things that you love and doing them whenever you need an extra relaxation boost can support you greatly in letting go of your deep attachment to worry and giving yourself the space that you need to actually enjoy life again.

This can be anything from using your favorite bath products in the shower each morning, to brewing your favorite coffee, or going to your favorite place that brings you peace. It can be different for different people. Take an inventory of the things that help promote peace and relaxation within you, and make an effort to use those powerful tools to support you in retraining your brain to stop staying so addicted to worry, and just chill the frick out.

CHAPTER 8:

DELAYED RETURN ENVIRONMENT…
WHATEVER THAT IS…

Delayed return who? What? Where? I know, this is a strange name. At least to me it is. But hang in there with me for a second, because this can actually tell you a lot about yourself, your worry, and how to get a freaking grip already.

First, let's get to the bottom of what "delayed return environment" even means. The best way to tell you is by giving you an example, so let's get to it, shall we? Yes. We shall.

You may be sitting on the couch right now with your cat or dog curled up beside you. If not, you are at least familiar with this setting. Now, imagine that your cat or dog feels hungry. Upon noticing this feeling, they immediately get up, stretch, and head over to their food dish to gobble on some of their kibble. This is called immediate return environment. This is because little Roscoe noticed he was hungry and immediately fulfilled his need.

You, on the other hand, might choose to binge watch three more episodes of Netflix or go through six more chapters of this incredibly enthralling book before actually getting up to eat. This would be delayed return environment. Most of the things that humans receive are benefits that are received with a delay. For example, if you work for an employer, you will most likely wait for two weeks for your paycheck rather than simply receiving it immediately for services rendered.

You may also have a retirement account that you drop funds into on a monthly basis so that when you retire, you have a nest egg to keep you from living under a bridge in your latter years. You may want to lose ten pounds, so you go and get on a treadmill for a half hour, yet you don't lose ten pounds instantaneously. (And if you do, please tell me your secret.) Most of the things that you do will not produce immediate benefits, hence the name delayed return environment.

Even though this is the type of society that we live in, it is actually not optimal for our mental health. On a biological level, we are still wired to expect and even need that immediate return environment. Does the phrase "instant gratification" ring a bell? Most people talk about it as though it is some terrible infection millennials have because they are glued to their phones all the time and throw fits whenever they have to wait longer than 2.5 milliseconds for anything.

The reality is, however, that this is actually what our brains are biologically wired to do. Anyone who speaks about instant gratification like they don't enjoy it or seek it in their own lives is lying to you. Every single human in existence loves and seeks out instant gratification because it feeds the brain's biological need to experience instant return environment.

Living in a delayed return environment stimulates greater stress and anxiety for humans. And not just because you are trying to ration your food between now and your next pay day, either. The biggest stress that really comes into play here is the fact that when we live in a delayed return environment, we live our entire lives feeling a deep sense of uncertainty. Because there is no guarantee that our actions will even pay off the way we expect them to, we begin to experience fear and stress.

For example, say you go to college and accrue tens or even hundreds of thousands of dollars in student loan debt in order to get that expensive and highly regarded degree. (If this is your real life story and I hit a sore spot, I apologize.) Even though you have a greater chance of finding a decent, good paying job, there is no guarantee. For that reason, your education can bring you great stress—not just because the studying is hard, but also because you have no idea as to whether or not it will even pay off in the end. The desired result of getting a high paying job that will afford you the ability to pay off the debt is not guaranteed.

The same goes for most things that we do in the modern world. For example, if you invest in a stock portfolio, there is no guarantee that it will increase. Heck, it might even decrease depending on the particular investment you have chosen. Going out on dates does not guarantee that you will find the soulmate that you have dreamt about your entire life. Going out on dates doesn't even guarantee that the person you're going out with will look like their profile picture. Even spending a significant amount of time making your favorite recipe that looked so easy and delicious on Pinterest does not guarantee that it will be easy or delicious. There is a great deal of uncertainty and thus worry and stress that comes from living in a society that is built around a delayed return environment.

But despite this, there are a great number of people who are actually thriving in our delayed return environment. So, what do they have that you don't?

Why the heck are they thriving while the rest of us are out here chewing our fingernails down to our knuckles?

The secret is measurement. Those who are thriving are measuring things to create some level of certainty in their lives. For example, if you are saving for your retirement, you may live in chronic fear that you will never have enough and therefore you will never be able to retire. A way of reducing this fear, eliminating uncertainty, and putting your mind at ease would be to measure what you are hoping or expecting to have.

Calculate how much you are putting away each month and discover how much you would have saved by the time you are ready to retire. Then, you can go ahead and work towards this plan in peace, knowing that if you do your part and meet your measurements, and hit your pre-determined increments and milestones, you will accomplish your goal. If you have any concerns or doubts about this amount, you can begin problem solving because now the problem is tangible and you have numbers directly in front of you that you can work with to create a solution that works. Having a solution puts your mind at ease, thus reducing the amount of stress that you experience in your life.

Another thing that you can do is to shift your worry. Instead of focusing on the things that you cannot control, begin focusing on the things that you can. This may seem extremely straightforward and simple, but it has a massive impact on your ability to genuinely feel better. For example, say you are worried that you are putting on too much weight. Rather than living in fear or setting a long term goal to lose weight, maybe it's easier for you to focus on eating healthier and cutting back 200 calories each day. Keeping your focus on small, simple, tangible, measurable things that you can do immediately will support you in finding peace by incorporating the feeling of immediate return environment into your delayed return environment world.

CHAPTER 9:

WORRYING CAUSES....
WAIT FOR IT...WAIT FOR IT...

Stress. Worrying causes stress. Mic drop. The lessons on stress, cortisol, adrenaline and worry are all still super fresh in your mind. At least, I hope they are. For that reason, we are not going to walk back down that science-y road. Instead, we are going to get down and dirty with some real-life examples and explanations regarding how your worry is increasing the stress in your life. It's time to get psychological about this.

Let's walk through a quick example of what happens when you worry on a psychological level. It starts with something arising that you feel the need to worry about. Maybe you have an important work deadline coming up and you are not sure that you are going to make it. So, you begin to worry that you will disappoint your boss. The worry intensifies as time ticks on and your deadline draws nearer. Even though you are actually almost done, the fear of not making it in time scares you. Maybe you remember the last time that you were slightly behind schedule and your boss reprimanded you harshly for your tardiness. You certainly do not want to experience their wrath again! So, you worry.

We have a tendency to believe that by fixating ourselves on what we are afraid of or by worrying that we will somehow be able to have greater control over the situation. This gives us a false sense of being able to prevent bad things from happening. But this fixation on the fear-inducing or worry-inducing situation actually results in us moving into greater states of worry. We begin catastrophizing.

In other words, we begin to believe that the worst-case scenario is going to happen, and we prepare for the future as though we have already in some way been able to guarantee that it would happen. It is not just enough to catastrophize about one worst-case scenario, though. We would of course be susceptible to other potential worst-case scenarios. Therefore, we begin to imagine all of the bad things that we believe will happen if we are not successful in preventing them somehow. This results in even more extensive worrying.

This type of extensive and catastrophic worrying is all-consuming. When we do it, we literally take away from our quality of life because we cannot reasonably live with this much worry in our minds. We are so focused on the problem that we are worried about, that we do not have the time to do basic things like eating, taking a shower, or sleeping. We keep ourselves awake at night, searching for answers. We skip meals trying to make up for lost time. And we struggle to convince ourselves that anything else could possibly be more important than what we are worried about.

This is obviously extremely unhealthy. Once we reach this state where we are no longer taking care of ourselves, we begin maximizing the stress we experience within ourselves. Not only is the worry itself causing our stress hormones to skyrocket so that we have the capacity to enter "fight" mode, but we are also not taking proper care of our bodies. Exhaustion, hunger, and a lack of downtime all come together to produce even more stress. At this point, your body must produce unnaturally high levels of cortisol and adrenaline to keep you going because you are not providing it with the necessary mental, physical, and emotional fuel needed.

It may seem like a big jump to some but moving from a small amount of worry into catastrophic worry is a common daily occurrence for most people. In fact, hundreds of thousands of people who live with anxiety disorders experience this exact type of worrying and stress on a daily basis.

Having chronic worry in your mind is not only overwhelming and noisy but it is also damaging to your health and well-being. It is essential that you begin incorporating your daily meditation practices and relaxation practices so that you can slow down, release some of the worry, and stop stressing.

If you are having a particularly challenging time releasing worry, something you might consider doing is writing down all of the reasons why you are worried so that you can address them and understand them. Realizing what is causing your worry and having them out on paper gives you the opportunity to use your problem-solving skills to come up with a solution that will support you in releasing and minimizing your worry.

Then, you should craft a plan. This plan should be the one that you will use to support you in doing whatever needs to be done. For example, if you are worried about a holiday dinner and the family that you will see there, have a plan of how you are going to act in the situations that you are worried about so you can take your intangible worry and transform it into a tangible solution. If you know you're going to get asked again why you're 40 and still single by your great aunt with the mustache (who happens to also be single), have a plan for how you're going to deal with her. Now you do not need to worry that you will be caught unprepared.

Preparing appropriately and staying focused on your solutions will ensure that you can minimize your worry and lessen the stress that you experience in your mind and body. This will leave you with wide open spaces to begin filling with your positive vibes.

CHAPTER 10:

WOOSAH

When we are in a state of stress or panic, it is easy to believe that we can be calmed down by external sources. Many of us will feel like we will be happier, less stressed, or more at peace when or if some desired future outcome comes to fruition. For example, "I will feel less stressed about finances when I have $10,000 in my savings account." Or "I will feel less miserable about my love life when I finally go on a good first date." Sound familiar? These external emotional fuelers (we're going to call them fuelers if that's okay with you) are extremely counterintuitive to our desire to have more peace, less stress, greater happiness, or less misery.

Basing your happiness on conditions outside of yourself (and sometimes outside of your control) is ultimately one of the laziest stances you can take towards improving your own life. That's right. Lazy. Rather than taking action over what you can control and providing your own source of happiness, peace, joy, or satisfaction, you simply sit around and whine until someone or something else does it for you.

Instead of making your happiness conditional, based on other people and circumstances that you have no control over, you need to take matters into your own hands and do what you can to become happy and peaceful right now no matter what is or isn't going on in your life at the moment. One great way to do this is to self-soothe. I know it sounds like something rich housewives with no actual problems do to kill time and feel important in between stressful shopping sprees at Hermes, but being able to take care of yourself and your own emotions, especially when it comes to stress, is essential.

Not only will it stop you from generating much higher levels of worry when you are waiting for your desired outcomes to occur, but it will also provide you with tangible and effective opportunities to actually feel those great emotions without having to wait for that circumstance to be met, and will give you a way to feel good whether that desired outcome takes place or not.

Self-soothing can also be something we associate with children. We have children learn to self-soothe so that they can sleep on their own. However, we do not have conversations about the importance of learning to self-soothe to deal with our more complex emotions and feelings later on in our adult lives. Just because we do not talk about it much does not mean it is not important.

Learning to self-soothe requires consistent practice and the willingness to commit to your self-soothing rituals on a regular basis. At first, it may not completely work. This is just like when a baby begins to learn to self-soothe and it cries incessantly for quite some time because it is not yet sure how to do this and does not yet know that everything is going to be okay. Do not cry incessantly like a baby. I assure you—you can do this and everything is going to be okay. As you continue practicing, the time between your stress and your ability to successfully soothe yourself becomes shorter each time.

As an adult, there are many different self-soothing practices that you can use to minimize stress, anxiety, and worry so that you can feel relaxed in your muscles and your mind. These techniques are used essentially as a way to interrupt the overwhelmed flow of energy that you are experiencing during your panic attacks...or as we like to call them here: freak outs.

The following practices are great self-soothing techniques that you can begin using to relax your mind and body and pull yourself back out of stressful experiences. This does not mean that there will be zero stress in your body, but it will prevent you from experiencing excessive and overwhelming stress that does not actually serve you in being able to come up with solutions or move into necessary action.

Soothing The Senses

The first step in learning to self-soothe requires you to learn how you can self-soothe your senses. There are two ways that you can soothe the senses. One is quick and the other requires more time.

Using the quick practice is a great way to experience…well, quicker (but less) relief from bouts of stress that come on quick and heavy. For example, if you suddenly experience a major burst of stress, using this practice would be perfect to help calm you down and draw you back into a state of calmness.

The quick practice works by recognizing each of your five senses and using them to experience the environment around you. This gets you back out of your mind and into your body, which pulls you out of mentally absorbing yourself in your problems, and brings balance back to how you can approach your life.

You will use the quick practice by taking a moment to activate each of your senses.

Start by looking at something in your environment. Pick something that you can spend a few minutes studying. Say the name of the object in your mind and mentally list off the different characteristics of it, such as its color, shape, and texture. This takes care of your sense of sight. Then, go on to something that you can hear. Take notice of where it is coming from, what it is, and what the sound itself sounds like. Then, find something that you can smell. Again, take a few moments to identify the source of the smell, what it smells like, what it likely is, and how you would describe that smell to someone else. Then, move on to taste. If you do not notice any recognizable or outstanding tastes in your mouth, you can always pop a piece of gum, a mint, or a small hard candy into your mouth. Then, you can move on to feeling. Find something that you can touch and take some time to identify what you are touching, and what it feels like. This quick sensory scan is designed to ~~make you look and feel like an idiot~~ bring you into the present, and connect you to your body instead of keeping you preoccupied inside your mind.

The longer method of using your senses to relax requires you to invest more time into tapping into your senses. You may do this by emphasizing one single sense during your session, or you can incorporate many senses. If you have a specific sense that you find tends to relax you more than the others, such as sense of smell for instance, then you can begin by focusing on that sense alone. Otherwise, you can just use all of the senses. This method is great for regular stress maintenance, and this can also provide extra relaxation when you have been dealing with a particularly troubling time.

You want to do this practice by engaging in an activity that will activate and soothe the senses. So, for the sense of hearing, you might want to spend some time listening to your favorite music or going to your favorite nature spot that has beautiful sounds, such as a park with birds or squirrels. For best results, isolate this sense the best you can.

If you chose sound, find a place to be still, close your eyes, and concentrate solely on what you hear. For sight, you might spend some time at an art gallery looking at beautiful pictures, or out in nature looking around at the various plant and animal species that you come across. For scent, you might melt some candles, diffuse some essential oils, or spend some time in a fragrant garden. For taste, you might spend time eating your favorite meal and taking your time so that you taste every bite. (Binge eating your favorite meal does not count as self-soothing.) For touch, you might lay in a comfortable fresh bed with warm sheets fresh out of the dryer, or you might cuddle with a soft blanket, or get a massage. If you want to incorporate all of the senses, you might want to go to a spa or create your own home spa experience, incorporating all of the senses at the same time with a wonderful, relaxing ambiance.

Distraction

Using distraction as a method of self-soothing is highly beneficial, so long as you are not distracting yourself to the point of avoidance. If you use being distracted as a defense mechanism to avoid your situation altogether, this will do more harm than good. You won't be able to overcome the stress because you are not actually working towards a solution and the stress from your lack of progress and inaction will continue building in the background. In this case, distraction can become destructive. However, using distraction properly can support you in freeing your mind from excess stress in a way that allows you to resume focus on the problem at hand so you can formulate a solution from a clearer state of mind.

There are multiple ways to use the technique of distraction. Taking a short, timed break from your stressful situation to do something completely different is one of the best ways. For example, if work is stressful, you might take a fifteen minute break to go for a walk around the block, grab some coffee, do a crossword puzzle, or play a quick game on your phone.

Nothing self-soothes like a good round of Candy Crush. This will distract you from the stress for a short period of time so that you can clear your mind and resume your activity later with less stress clouding up your mental space.

It is important that you always schedule when you are going to return to the original activity, and then follow through on the schedule that you set. That bears repeating—it is important that you always schedule when you are going to return to the original activity, and then follow through on the schedule that you set. Not doing so will not only get you off track in completing your task at hand, but will also take you down a negative spiral of disappointment in yourself over your lack of discipline and will power.

So, whether you decide on fifteen minutes, a few hours, a couple of days, or even a couple of weeks of break (depending upon what makes sense for the situation), make sure that you set a specific return time so that your stress reliever doesn't end up just creating more stress for you. Make sure that this return time still gives you plenty of time to complete whatever needs to be accomplished of your original task. If you take a break with no limitation on how long the break will last, it becomes easier to turn distraction into avoidance, causing you to experience greater stress because you are no longer facing your troubles but are ignoring them instead.

Light Exercising

Moving your body around can have a profound impact on getting yourself relaxed. Things like yoga, water aerobics, and other gentle exercises you may think are reserved for soccer moms, men with ponytails, or senior citizens can be very effective. These gentle exercises are relaxing enough to calm your mind, but active enough to move stress through you so that it can be released. Having a regular exercise practice can support you in feeling less stressed out by the circumstances in your life. It is also a great way to seek refuge from spikes of stress that may cause you to feel overwhelmed or trapped in worry.

It is worth noting that when you are self-soothing, it is a good idea to refrain from excessive exercise. High endurance exercise activities can actually increase your stress hormones, so it is a good idea to avoid these if you want to uh...decrease your stress hormones.

CHAPTER 11:

HOW TO SLEEP WITH
A BRAIN FULL OF...

I think you know where I'm going with that. Let's face it—sleeping is really freaking hard when you are stressed, worried, and your brain is wracked with reasons to freak out. There are usually two tendencies when we try to sleep when we are stressed. Either you sleep more than usual and you still feel exhausted or you don't sleep at all. If you are barely sleeping at all, the idea of getting any sleep seems impossible. If you are sleeping more than usual, getting a rest that actually feels refreshing seems impossible. Sound about right?

Still, sleep is essential, so we need to do something about it.

The big problem?

Bedtime is when worries start to really kick in. You know the drill. Your head hits the pillow, you close your eyes, and instead of lovely images of counting sheep, all the reminders of everything you ever did wrong in your life and everything you're convinced you will do wrong in your life flood into your brain, leaving you stuck with another restless night. You might even become so worried that when you do finally fall asleep, you actually wake yourself up. Not only does this level of worry disrupt your sleep, but this lack of sleep heightens your worry. So, which came first, the chicken or the egg? Truthfully, it doesn't matter. I just wanted to say that out loud.

Just because you have not yet found the solution to sleeping when you are worried does not mean the solution does not exist. Luckily, the answer is not in drinking gallons of chamomile tea and slathering yourself in all things lavender. In fact, there are many answers and each of them provides you with a great way to release the worry rather than simply avoiding the processing stage. Your sleep, which is naturally used to process unprocessed thoughts and emotions from your day, can be peaceful after all.

One great way to begin having a restful sleep each night is to set aside worrying time before you even get into bed. Rather than letting it all come crashing down on you the moment your head hits the pillow, sit somewhere away from your bed with a journal and dump all of your worrying thoughts out into the pages. Yup, time for that journal again. This does not have to be in any particular formal format, nor do you need to start each time you write in "dear diary" fashion. Don't stress about how you're going to de-stress!

Simply get these worries out, whether you write them word for word, stream of consciousness, jot them down in a bullet-point list, draw stick figures, whatever you need to do, just get it on paper so you can remove it from your psyche. The idea here is to create a contained environment and block of time where you literally let yourself worry. There is absolutely no need to try and pull yourself back in with anti-worrying techniques. This is not the time to self-soothe. This is not the time to light your incense. Instead, set a timer and let yourself go. Allowing yourself to be consumed by worrying gives yourself an honest chance to process all of the thoughts and emotions that you are feeling. When you get your worries on paper, you'll likely see that you have no control over many of the things you're worrying about, or you may find that they're not likely to happen, or not as bad as you think.

Another thing you can do is to stop actually trying to sleep. Forget all of the practices you have heard about. Forget about the different teas, tinctures, vitamins, herbs, and rah-rah practices you can use to get yourself to sleep. Instead, just stop trying to sleep and focus on releasing your anxiety. When the anxiety itself is released, the sleep will come naturally.

Meditation practices are also known to be great before bedtime, but starting a practice from scratch as a way to get yourself to sleep is likely not helpful. The earliest stages of learning to meditate can be frustrating because we are so used to being wound up stress balls and being wired for worry. Trying to go against the grain of biology can be frustrating and can actually result in you stressing yourself out more. If you already meditate on a regular basis, incorporating a bedtime meditation practice into your routine can be helpful. Otherwise, if you have been attempting to cultivate a practice before bed without any pre-established practice, it may be a good idea to abandon this for now.

Another thing that you can do for yourself when you are attempting to restore your sleep schedule so that you can feel rested in the morning is actually to allow yourself to feel. Similar to the idea of setting aside worrying time, try putting your emphasis on feeling through your anxiety rather than shoving it aside.

There are several moments when we are so unwilling to face worry and anxiety because it can generate such massive amounts of fearful, negative energies within us. As a result, we end up denying it and, in many cases, it simply builds up and becomes even more challenging for us to face. Furthermore, we then have to train ourselves to stop denying it and this can make it even more difficult to even recognize it, never mind feeling our way through it.

Rather than attempting to use a one-size-fits-all practice that will quickly cast your feelings aside, consider just simply feeling them instead. In most cases, emotions that are adequately felt and processed will subside and you can move on to enjoy your regular life. Emotions that are repressed and not processed, however, will compound and turn into stress—the very stress that keeps you up at night and makes you feel tired and groggy in the morning.

Part 3:

This Is
The Third Part

CHAPTER 12:

OH, THE IRONY

It's a bit insane to realize that the very purpose of fear itself is to serve us in self-preservation, yet it can be a life sucking, all-consuming, just not fun, negative force. Still, we experience fear on a regular basis. In fact, many of us experience fear on a constant basis. This is because despite our lives being advanced, our bodies have yet to evolve enough to actually catch up. In some ways, we're still cavemen, remember?

Even in our modern society, fear can serve a great purpose. However, the way fear presents itself in our bodies and minds still suggests that it is attempting to save us from being hunted, rather than things that are actually relevant to today's times. We become hyper stressed when faced with uncertainty. On a biological level, the fear we experience when "modern day" bad things happen (say the coffee pot is empty and we do not have enough time to make one before we leave), it actually triggers a stress and fear response similar to the feeling of being hunted by a man-eating tiger. More drastic experiences, such as watching the news and learning of a natural disaster for example, can trigger a response of fear that is so great that we may literally feel like we are in the middle of a forest, cornered against a tree by a predator.

Very few of us are actually taught how to manage fear and use it productively. In our collective defense, it is a challenge to use self-preservation instincts in a way that is helpful to us. It doesn't take long for self-preservation to turn into self-destruction.

See, self-preservation is intended to teach you to avoid all measures of pain. In an immediate return environment (as experienced by animals), this would be easy and makes perfect sense. Outside of literally being eaten, the lifestyle animals live does not generally require them to endure any degree of physical, mental, or emotional pain. For them, self-preservation is still for just that—saving their lives. Say a squirrel is running too fast through the trees and misses a branch and falls, for example. Self-preservation would instinctively teach this squirrel to change his technique to refrain from falling in the future. The squirrel is not losing sleep at night, however, replaying over and over again in his head how he missed that branch or how he's such a screw that he'll probably miss a branch again tomorrow because he sucks at life. His self-preservation instinct helps him adjust his behavior in the moment to ensure his survival, which makes perfect sense in an immediate return environment.

In a delayed return environment, however, you have already learned that there are varying degrees of stress and pain that we are not biologically wired for. This means that self-preservation actually creates more harm than good. Our constant failure to experience instant gratification in our needs or desires being met results in self-preservation techniques such as fear skyrocketing and causing us to become excessively worried. Furthermore, we also experience pains that most animals do not tend to experience such as rejection, embarrassment, and shame.

As a result, there are many different factors in our everyday lives that trigger our self-preservation instincts to kick off, and we end up finding ourselves huddled in the corner, chewing on our own hair in the fetal position, muttering "What am I doing with my life?" Or something like that.

Not only does it create intense fear that can cause us to become self-destructive, but this particular self-preservation instinct can also cause a whole slew of other problems. For example, say you are afraid that you will fail at something or embarrass yourself if you try it. Suddenly, your self-preservation instinct kicks in and boom, you are not even willing to try anymore. Now, you won't get to experience the potential success or self-esteem boost that could have been on the other side because you never even allowed yourself to go for it.

Overcoming instincts can be a challenge, but it is not necessarily impossible. It requires a significant effort put into brain strength training that will allow you to consciously step into your conscious thinking mind during these periods of fear and override your instinct. Sounds very bionic, huh?

By using critical thinking within your conscious mind, you can literally challenge your natural instincts, deem them false, and then consciously tell your mind to reduce the production of adrenaline and other fear-related hormones within your body. This is another great form of self-soothing, by the way.

By regularly challenging that little voice inside that constantly tells you that you are going to die or be seriously hurt if you do anything, ever, you give yourself the opportunity to actually overcome these fears and stop your self-preservation from turning into self-destruction. Using those daily habits from Chapter 6 can help you experience the magic of evolution in action and get your body to catch up biologically from those caveman days. Challenging that nasty voice and telling it to shut the hell up already, then going on to actually shut it up and override it with a positive voice is pretty freaking epic. Not to mention that it will change your life.

REESE OWEN

CHAPTER 13:

IT'S NOT YOU, IT'S THEM

Well…it's partially you. You're not completely off the hook, but here's another good old fashioned scapegoat for you that should make you feel better—you are the way you are partially because of the people you are surrounded by. I'm sure you've heard that you are the average of your five closest friends. And I'm sure growing up, you heard at some point in your childhood some adult that you didn't want to listen to tell you that you are the company you keep.

Allow me to be that adult from your childhood. You are the company you keep. If you want to shut up that inner mean voice once and for all (which you do because you got this book), you need to remove all of the toxicity from your life. You can do affirmations and tell yourself you're a badass until you're blue in the face, but if you are still surrounded by toxicity, that inner mean voice is going to come right back. Negativity feeds negativity. If you starve it, it will die. But if it is fed by other negative people, that inner negative voice will survive, thrive, and take over. Furthermore, outside negativity and toxicity will only prove to your inner mean voice that it is right, thus giving it evidence and fuel to validate the lies it tells you about yourself and your life.

The people you spend the most of your time with reflect back on you in a big way. Not only do they influence how you behave and think, but they also show you who you are, which, depending on who you spend your time with, might be a little freaky.

Spending your time with the wrong people can influence you to have a toxic outlook in life. However, you can also identify where that toxicity is seeping in from so that you can repair the boat before it sinks. It is important that you take a few moments to recognize who you are spending your time with and to critically analyze them. It may seem a little strange to go all Judge Judy on your friends and start analyzing them under a microscope, but it is truly important if you are going to begin understanding who you are, why you behave and think in a certain way, how you can begin changing, and who you want to become.

When you start looking closely at your circle, you are going to notice one of two things: The person will either prove to be a positive influence that makes you feel uplifted after being around them, or you will begin to recognize that they are extremely toxic, and they seem to bring you down every time you spend time together. If they are toxic, you may even be able to tap into some self-awareness here and begin to see how you may share the same toxic behaviors as they do. If your company is toxic, you can pretty much guarantee that you are as well. As much as we may not want to admit it, the people around us can be mirrors to ourselves. Identifying how the negative people around you are toxic can help you identify the same in yourself.

Once you have separated your "keepers" from your "Debbie downers," it is time to get into action by cleaning out your friends list and creating sacred space for you to feel good. This friends list goes both ways: online and offline. Keeping toxic people out of your space altogether is essential as it refrains from them having any hold over you. Many people believe that they can tone down personal interactions but can tolerate toxic people in social media. This is false. What you likely do not realize is that even if you do not talk to them or associate with them, you will censor yourself, judge yourself, and otherwise adjust your online behavior to accommodate for what you believe they would think of you if you were to behave like a nontoxic, non-GMO human. For real.

Getting toxic people out of your space can feel scary, especially if they are people whom you are particularly close to. There is almost nothing harder than having to break up with a life-long friend or reduce the amount of time you spend around family members because they are too toxic and they add more stress in your life. But, on the flip side, there is also nothing greater than waking up in the morning and going about your day without the negativity and pessimism of toxic people sloshing about in your life, dragging you down, and robbing you from just having a good day.

If you are peering through the microscope and wondering what the heck you are looking for when choosing who to weed out of your life, the answer is quite simple: you are looking for signs that the person is filled with negativity and pessimism and that they show no signs of trying to change. Those friends of yours who are negative but who are neck-deep in self-help books are probably great to keep around, so long as they are taking action on what they are learning. They will actually understand what you are going through and you can support each other along the way. They are the only exception you get when it comes to keeping negative people around.

Negative people who are completely oblivious to their negativity are the ones that you have to look out for. You know their type. The kind of people that sit around bitching endlessly about everything from their mundane work life, to the color of someone's toenails, or the end results in a sports game sixteen years ago. They almost never say anything polite, their compliments are usually backhanded, manners elude them, and they are still dwelling on shitty events that had nothing to do with them from decades past. These are the type of people that you can assume are toxic and that you need to avoid.

If you need a cheat sheet, you should be cautious of anyone who is:

- Overly judgmental
- A bully
- Harshly critical
- Lacks basic manners and social skills
- Takes advantage of you or others
- Disrespects their Mamma (or dad)
- Lacks consideration for others
- Frequently skips out on your time together
- Fails to call you when plans change or when they'll be late
- Otherwise behaves in a way that makes you feel worse than a post-rave hangover.

Although you may want to try to be the voice of reason here, and go on about how being positive means seeing the best in others, I have to stop you right there in your tracks. Yes, it is always a good thing to see the best in others. No, this does not mean every other person is good company. Just because people have flaws and faults does not necessarily mean that they are bad people. Rather, it means that they are bad people to keep around.

You're a ball of stress, remember? And you're trying to turn your life around, remember? It's bad enough that you're jumping out of your britches in panic at the "out of order" sign on the drive-thru machine but having someone who constantly drags you down with negativity is more than anyone can reasonably handle. This is a great time to apply the "love from a distance" practice to these relationships by limiting the amount of time you spend with these people or by removing them from your life altogether.

You are not a bad person for wanting to keep your life and time available for being positive and for other people who are positive as well. This does not mean that you are better or holier than those people are, and you never experience a bad day or you never bitch about the fact that the coffee was empty yet again on your break at work today. What it does mean is that you choose not to spend every single waking minute concerned and worried about these things. Instead, you like to, you know, laugh once in a while. And you are not selfish for wanting to do so, either.

Also, make sure that once you eliminate these people from your life, you do not suddenly get overcome with worry, guilt, and more stress and then go right back to hanging out with them. You have to go cold turkey here, my friend. Say it with me--no takesies backsies. Jumping back into a toxic relationship because you are afraid of hurting someone else's feelings will do you no good. Be selfish. Cut the ties and then hit a Paint n' Sip class or the local activity center (whatever that is) and find yourself some new, wholesome friends who will be happy to laugh with you.

CHAPTER 14:

CHANNELING YOUR INNER ROCKET

Do you remember what they say when a rocket ship launches? "10... 9... 8... 7... 6... 5... 4... 3... 2... 1... BLAST OFF!" Right? Good. You are about to launch yourself like a NASA spacecraft and get your ass off the couch and actually do something about your life. Seriously, today is the day that you are going to stop bitching about all of the things that have gone wrong in your life and you are going to make some serious changes.

You have already read this far. You know about all of the fancy science-y words and phrases like cortisol, delayed return environment, and negativity bias. You have thought about them, probably begun to recognize them in your life, and likely even snickered at yourself when you caught yourself mentally judging the crap out of—well, everything in the past several days. But I would be willing to believe that you have not yet entirely committed to your life-changing action yet, have you? You know why? One word my friend: instant gratification.

There is a good chance that as soon as you read Chapter 6, you excitedly jumped into action and began all of your daily practices. Then, around three to seven days later, you had either completely forgotten all about them or you were so upset that they were not producing instant results that you gave up. Right? I am right, aren't I? I'm usually always right.

That is your brain at work again. You are looking for instant gratification. You are looking for present results, and a brand new life handed to you on a silver platter with a little after-dinner mint on the side, aren't you? Typical millennial. At least that's what the baby boomers always say. If you are a millennial, don't let them be right about the "problem with your generation."

I'm calling it. The time is now. You need to get off your couch, get into action, and begin taking the steps to actually change your life. You can read as many books, blogs, and inspirational quotes as you want, but if you never actually do something about any of it, you will never actually quit your miserable life and start at your shiny new life of optimism and hurrah.

Here is what I want you to do: you are going to start by confronting yourself. Grab that journal of yours and write down all of the reasons why you have not yet started or stuck to your daily habits. Be brutally honest with yourself, there is no time for weakness or censorship here. You deserve the truth, the whole truth, and nothing but the truth. Tell yourself all the many reasons why you still suck. I'll wait.

Now, I would be willing to bet that one of the reasons that showed up on your list, if you were being truly honest with yourself, was that you were afraid that if you really put in a solid effort, you would still not see any results from your actions. I want you to go ahead and confront this particular fear right here, right now. This is where you are going to grab some motivation to truly get your ass up and make changes. I want you to explain to yourself why you are afraid of failing, and what failing would mean to you. I also want you to explain to yourself why succeeding means so much to you that you are literally frozen with fear. (Damn self-preservation instincts, at it again!)

Getting a clear understanding on how much this actually means to you will have a massive impact on helping you truly recognize why you want this so much. Now you have a tangible understanding of what is at stake if you fail, and you can clearly see in front of you, plain as day, why you are so dead set on succeeding with your life-changing habits.

Next, you need to let yourself off the hook. You are biologically wired to limit yourself and avoid positive and productive action, remember? Drop the woe-is-me act and place the blame where it really belongs: on your biology. Then, place the responsibility where it really belongs: on your conscious thinking mind. It may be your biology that has gotten you to this point, but now that you know better, it is time for your conscious mind to step in, shut the party down, and get on with business. Passing blame back and forth and refusing to take any serious action is never going to get you anywhere. You need to take conscious responsibility and be willing to take conscious action, too. There is no room for "Sorry, but I'm probably going to do that sucky thing that gets me nowhere again today" types of apologies and excuses. Your biology owes your conscious mind an apology, and your conscious mind owes your biology some forgiveness.

Lastly, I want you to make a plan on how you are going to stay committed. Set a reminder in your phone, buy sixty-two calendars and place them all over your house, get a buddy to do this "new life" thing with you, or set an old school alarm clock next to your bed that is going to remind you that it is time to take action. Using tools like this to relieve yourself from biology kicking in and dragging you back into the pit of laziness is essential. If you really want to give your conscious mind a fighting chance at helping you out of this nasty pit you have dug yourself into, you need to make sure that you are consciously coming up with a way to stay in your conscious mind. (If it were easy, you wouldn't be reading this book now, would you?)

With that being said, it is time for you to get to action. Start setting yourself up for success by setting these reminders in place and keeping Chapter 6 handy to help you get into the routine of practicing your daily positivity habits. You can also set up intermittent reminders that literally remind you to check yourself (before you wreck yourself). If you have anything else that you love to add in to your own routines that help you feel supported, positive, and a whole heck of a lot less worried, do not be afraid to add those in, too. Remember, it is you that you are trying to impress here, not me. Go all in and woo yourself like you have never been wooed before. You deserve it.

Ready?

10... 9... 8... 7... 6... 5... 4... 3... 2... 1... BLAST OFF!

CHAPTER 15:

MORE WOOSAH

You didn't think that you were going to get away from this with a simple "take a nice bath and smell the roses" list, did you? After all, this book is about learning how to ditch your inner worrywart and begin living an ultra-zen(ish) life, right?

I thought so.

Practicing any and all relaxation strategies is important. Sensual baths, smelling roses, massages, and going for a good walk in nature are all wonderful ways to relax yourself. But they are not always enough. Sometimes, you need more. Sometimes, you need unusual. Sometimes, your brain does not register anything when you hear advice like that because you feel like you've been there, done that, and have a souvenir keychain to mark the memory with too.

Here are some practices that you can use that are relaxing, a bit out-there (like, space alien out there), but extremely effective. Using these practices can help you snap out of a bout of worry, or just increase your relaxation drive to max level. They are unusual. You have been warned.

- **Read A Book Out Loud**

Reading has long been known as being a greatly relaxing activity for people to engage in. Losing yourself in a book where the character's life is much better than yours (or worse, depending on what you are into) can be extremely helpful in distracting you from your own crummy reality. However, when you are particularly worried and stressed out, there is a good chance that you will not actually absorb what you are reading. Thus, it can become incredibly boring or it may not help at all.

Instead, grab your favorite book and read it out loud. Narrate the book in a theatrical way, give the characters unique voices, and get artistic with the process. Engaging yourself in the book this way is both distracting, and enjoyable. If you have kids, you can even grab some of their favorite books and read to them in this way. Not only can you bond with your kiddos, you'll feel entertained in the process and be far less worried about the craziness going on in your life right now.

- **Walk Sideways**

For real. Instead of going for a regular walk, go shuffle sideways down the sidewalk. Not only is this a great cardio workout but it also requires a lot of focus and physical activity. It also decreases stress because it is literally one repetitive motion. You'll be getting movement into muscles that you are less likely to use on a regular basis; this means that your physical body is "alert" in a way that it is not used to being alert. It is a great way to pull you out of your noisy mind and get you moving while also distracting you from the chaos you are thinking about. Just make sure you don't trip!

- **Have A Themed Hangout**

Remember when you were like five, and your best friend had a princess or race car themed birthday, and everyone got to dress up in themed party hats and play games that were aligned with the party theme?

It's time to bring back the good ol' days and plan yourself a themed hangout. Get together a group of your friends and plan to hang out with any theme you desire. This could be anything from a Hawaiian theme to a space craft theme. Be creative and get into character. Dress up, drink themed drinks, eat themed snacks, say themed things, and have fun doing activities that align with your theme as well. Getting your mind distracted with some good, wholesome fun and sharing the fun with those you love is a great way to overcome excessive worry and infuse more fun into your life. Seriously, who couldn't use more fun in their life?

- **Play Pretend While Doing Yard Work**

Carrying on with the play pretend train, let's move on to another fun thing that you can do: play pretend while doing yard work. Yard work itself is believed to be a stress reliever because it gets you back in touch with nature. And supposedly sixteen pounds of dirt under your fingernails and a gallon of sweat dripping down your back is relaxing. At least, that is what they say.

But what if you switch it up a little? Instead of doing yard work in general, pretend you are a world-famous horticulturist and you have just discovered a brand new plant species. See where the fun brings you. Is it a bird? Is it a plane? No! It is a common fern, and I just freakin' discovered it for the first time ever! A Bloom Award, for me?? My, my! You bet your sweet ass I'll accept it! I'd like to thank my friends and my family for always supporting me...

You get the point.

- **Be A Backup Dancer In A Music Video**

Dancing is an amazing cardio workout that can also work out the anxiety from your body. But let's be honest, dancing to some music can be hard to motivate yourself to do sometimes. Especially when you are wretched with worry and stress. Even though it is known to be a great practice, not many people can actually "act as if" and dance around their house like a seizing gorilla until they feel good.

So, what if you weren't you anymore? What if you were one of the backup dancers from the video?

Throw on some music, better yet a music video, and get dancing as if you are actually in it. Throw your feet around, push that booty back, and wave your hands in the air like you just don't care. Because, let's be honest, you probably don't. And that's a great thing, if you think about it. No cares equal no worries!

- **Play With Your Kids**

Once again, I'm assuming you're a millennial, since your Grandma probably wouldn't pick up a book called Bitch, Don't Kill My Vibe. That said, first things first, let's release the stress around the fact that as millennials we are already old enough to have kids! Who let that happen, right?! Frickin time, man. Frickin. Time.

But seriously, kids are an amazing stress reliever if you let them be. I know you might think of your sweet darling children and recall having to shout at them forty-seven times on the way to the car so that they would get their shoes on and another seventy-two times on the way to school so they would put them back on before you reached the school parking lot. But truly they are wonderful at helping us release worry and stress from our lives when we are not actually trying to get anything done with them.

If you have kids, head into your child's bedroom (or playroom if you've got it like that) and offer to play with them. Even if you only hang out for fifteen minutes, letting your inhibitions wander away and playing with your children is a great way to overcome any stress or worry you are experiencing. Once you are done, you will likely feel much better after awakening your inner child.

And if you don't have kids, borrow some. I'm sure there are countless numbers of overworked, overstressed parents who would love to loan you their children for a few hours (or longer) so they can have time to take one of those sensual baths, or walk sideways.

- **Play With Your Pets**

Pets have an incredibly healing aura. Spending time with animals is a great way to either just cuddle and relax as you let your fears melt away, or actually get out, get physical, and play with them. Animals have been known to support humans in relaxing for many different reasons. Hence the abundance and variety of service animals nowadays.

Playing with your pet by throwing the ball around, getting down and wrestling with them, or otherwise just enjoying their presence is a great way to throw caution to the wind and have some good old-fashioned fun. Make sure that you really give over to it and break your attention from your worrying so that you can have fun. As a bonus, it will increase your bond with Fido and make them happier, too.

- **Cook With Mystery Ingredients**

This unique idea is a great way to have fun while also getting a (hopefully) tasty meal out of the deal. You know the drill: you watch Iron Chef for seven hours on your day off and then you are completely ready to create your own masterpiece that would be worthy of a prize. Even if that prize is for ugliest and worst tasting dish on the table.

A great way to release your worries, have some fun, and enjoy some relaxation is to go into your fridge and pantry and pick out random ingredients. Then, challenge yourself to make a dish using all of these ingredients. Spending time finding a recipe, chopping, sautéing and otherwise prancing around the kitchen like you are a professional is a great way to enjoy yourself. Plus, when you eat the dish in the end you get to enjoy a great sensory experience that can even further relax you.

- **Meditate Naked**

Here's a new one for you. You have already read about meditating half a million times, but have you ever heard of meditating naked? Meditating naked is a great way to help you become one with your own body. In addition, it is a completely unusual sensation; therefore, it will actually support you in drawing your awareness and attention to your body rather than merely attempting to meditate while getting distracted by all of the things that have been stressing you out to begin with.

The key here is to make sure that you have absolutely nothing on. And no one around. And that you have a comfortable surface to sit on. And your blinds are closed. (You don't want anyone peering in for a free show now, do you?) Let your mind clear itself and relax into the experience. Not only will this allow you to stay focused and actually relax, but it will also support you in having a better relationship with your body. Getting used to the feeling of being naked is a great way to feel confident in your nakedness and love yourself as you are.

- **Do Something Completely Unusual For You**

Nothing will pull your mind out of a rank funk better than doing something completely different than your norm. Chances are you have a (boring) routine that you do day in and day out. Correct me if I am wrong, but it probably looks something like this: wake up, get ready, drag your feet to work, barely get the job done, head home, watch Netflix, eat supper, go to sleep, repeat. Right? Oh, and of course you have weekends. During your weekends you likely wake up, do nothing, complete a bunch of adulty errands, do nothing, and then go to sleep.

So, instead of carrying on with your boring life that has gotten you nowhere, how about try doing something completely out of the usual for you. Hit the town, go to karaoke night (and actually get up there and sing), head to a carnival and hop on a ride, see a movie, go pet a bunch of animals at a local petting farm, or watch a tiger lounge around at the zoo. Find something to do that is far from usual for you, let go of your inhibitions, and give yourself a chance to really enjoy it.

The more you find ways to allow yourself to step outside of the nitty-gritty and too-serious ways of modern life and actually invest yourself in having fun and enjoying your life, the better you are going to feel. Sometimes, relaxing is not all about having smelly lotion on your feet and a cold cucumber water in your hand. Sometimes it is about stepping away from reality and letting loose for a while. Give yourself a chance to be free and enjoy life once more and you will find that relaxing and letting go of anxiety, stress and worry becomes much easier.

Bragging on the internet can sometimes
be a good thing.

This is one of those times.

Leave a review on Amazon, bragging about
how awesome you are for reading this book.

Part 4:

This Is The Only Part
That Actually
Has A Name—
The New You…
Woo-Hoo!

CHAPTER 16:

GETTING COMFY IN YOUR SKIN

Go look in the mirror right now. Hurry, do it! What do you see? ("Me, duh!") No really, look deeper. What do you see? Are you happy with what, or rather who you are looking at? Are you comfortable being you? Or do you struggle to accept the face (or body) looking back at you?

What are you thinking when you think about yourself? Are you proud of all you are achieving by taking daily action toward having a less stressed life, or are you finding yourself judging you based on who you were before you started these life-changing habits?

As humans, we have a hard time staying "up to date" on the latest and greatest versions of ourselves. Often, we form an attachment to one of our identities of times past and use that as the lens through which we see ourselves today. Of course, due to negativity bias and self-preservation, we usually cling to a negative image of ourselves. One that includes us not living up to our potential, not following through on improving ourselves, or behaving in ways that made us feel shameful. This is because by holding on to a memory of this identity, we can remind ourselves about the pain it brought us and why we do not want to do these things again. Except, generally it just results in us doing them again and again anyways because that is how we identify, so we do not tend to hold ourselves to any higher of standards or believe a Me 2.0 is possible.

But alas—step aside, outdated identity! It is time to recognize that you are updating your operating system. There is a new you in town and they are here to stay! You are no longer the old, rusty, rickety version of you that drove you crazy. You are the version of you who is determined to find solutions and love yourself in spite of everything you have experienced and everything you have done in your life. You are finding the answer to self-love through the art of quitting your addiction to worry and shutting up that nasty inner voice.

Getting used to this new you can take some time. However, it is essential that you take the time to warmly welcome them and invite them into your space. Get to know the new you and spend time discovering exactly who you are. Letting yourself get to know the new and improved version of yourself can support you in letting go of the identity that you previously held on to. This is where you can begin getting comfortable in your own skin as you now, not you before.

Spend some time really with yourself. Schedule some alone time (literally put it in your calendar), enjoy activities that you love by yourself, ask yourself questions, give yourself answers, journal, and really pick your own brain about who you are.

Getting comfortable in your own skin as a new version of you will most likely take time, but there are some practices that you can begin using to support you in achieving this as well. Spending time with yourself is a great one, but if you feel you need an extra boost, here are some other ideas that you can use to support you in this venture:

- **Compliment Your Naked Self In The Mirror**

Most people have a hard time complimenting themselves in general, never mind whilst naked in front of a mirror. However, actually giving yourself some time to compliment yourself to your own face in this vulnerable state is an incredible way to begin falling in love with you. Spend a few minutes before or after a shower, admiring yourself in the mirror, and let those compliments roll. If you find this to be challenging at first, focus on finding three things to compliment in one minute. Then, you can end your session. Increase your session and the amount of compliments you want to give yourself until you are easily finding (and comfortably receiving) numerous compliments. This will do a great number on helping you improve your self-love as well as your appreciation for your physical body.

- **Take An "Ultimate Get To Know Myself" Quiz And Answer Truthfully**

There are several times when we are not entirely comfortable with ourselves because we do not really know who we are. This can really hold us back from feeling comfortable in our own skin because we feel as though we are trapped in a body with a stranger. Getting to know yourself through solo activities like taking quizzes that ask you many personal questions, and enjoying your favorite group activities alone (i.e. go to a yoga class where you do not know anyone) is a really great way to get to know yourself more.

Think of your best friend, for example. You have likely spent so much time with them that you know things about them that no one else would. You could go to their favorite restaurant and order their favorite meal for them, complete with all the annoying modifications they would make. You know where they hide their favorite cup so guests don't accidentally use it. You know what books they would add to their cart on Amazon. And you know where they keep the gum in their car. You probably know what their relationship status with their parents is and why, what their darkest secrets are, and what they are afraid of. In some cases, you may even know more about them than they do because you spend so much time observing them. Getting to know yourself more on this intimate level will help you feel like your own best friend.

- **Affirm Your Love for Yourself Daily**

This particular subject populates nearly every self-help list that ever existed, so we do not need to go too much into detail. However, it is important to echo the fact that affirming your love for yourself on a daily basis is important. Reminding yourself of this, especially when you need it most (which is typically when it feels hardest to say) is important.

- **Stand Up for Yourself**

Standing up for yourself is a great way to really affirm your self-love through action. You should advocate for yourself not only in social situations with other people, but also toward yourself. Whenever you hear that inner mean voice growing audible, shut it up and stand up for yourself. Tell it that it has no business being rude and that if it has anything it wants to say it can say it nicely, otherwise it needn't say anything at all. Do not let it become your own worst nightmare and bully yourself senseless. Stand up for yourself and stand up with pride.

- **Learn Your Perfect Self-Care Routine**

There are probably a million self-care blog articles floating around ever since the blogging-for-money thing blew up back in the early 2000's. There is certainly no shortage of advice when it comes to finding great self-care strategies that you can use in your own life. From slathering your hair with strange ingredients like mayo and honey, and steeping in a bath filled with herbal teas, to yelling into pillows and taking up kick boxing, there are many different things you can find out there. Still, that does not mean that the seemingly perfectly curated self-care routines shared in these articles will actually help you.

Each individual is unique and thus has a unique set of desires, needs, and interests. Finding a self-care routine that actually checks all of your boxes is a great way to ensure that you actually feel relaxed and refreshed following the practice—whatever you decide that it is. In other words, if you throw up in the back of your mouth at the sound of the words "coconut oil" because you are so tired of reading about how it will cure you from…everything, skip over that and find yourself something more personalized. Having a proper routine that fits your needs, and accommodates for what actually relaxes you is essential. Plus, it will help you get to know yourself and feel more comfortable just that much more.

- **Focus On Healing**

It should go without saying that healing is an essential step in loving yourself and in increasing your relaxation. If you are a human, especially one with chronic stress and worry, you are carrying around baggage that has not yet been healed. You need to get on that.

Focusing on healing does not necessarily mean spending top dollar on the best therapists in the world so they can pick your brain and analyze you. Though, it might.

However, finding healing truly starts with setting the intention, feeling worthy of healing, and embarking on the journey that presents itself before you. When you ask to find healing, answers arise within you. If you look for it, you will find it. Seriously, it happens. It's like you are a magician or something. I think weird people call it like the law of attraction or something.

Opening your mind to a new you, free of all of the residual stress from your unhealed past, can help you not only feel more comfortable in your own skin, but it can also silence that negative inner voice and reduce a great deal of your stress.

- **Love Your Flaws**

Does your nose look like a toucan? Do you have legs taller than a palm tree? Does your hair hang strangely, making you look like a semi-shaved wet dog? Do your fingers bend in weird ways that make them resemble a crazy straw? Good. These are all indicative of you being a human. Not that all humans have large noses, long legs, strange hair, or crazy straw fingers. But all humans do have something that is just plain different about them. Those of us who are evolved enough to have grown to love our flaws call these differences character.

It is not unlikely that the reason you know that a part of your body is different is because someone so rudely pointed it out to you at least once in your lifetime. Comments like that stick. They make us feel like we are not normal. Biologically, it makes us fear that we will not be accepted into the tribe because we do not look like the others. (We are literally wired to prefer people that look like us. This is, however, no excuse for racism. Okay, I'm going to get back on track before I end up on a huge tangent cleverly disguised as a soapbox.)

You are perfectly normal if you have some trait about you that stands out quite obviously. You are also certainly going to be accepted by those who love you without them giving one care about this "flaw." In fact, they may not even notice it because most people are not looking. They're too busy worrying about their own flaws.

Learning to come to terms with and love your uniqueness on a physical level is very important. It all starts with one thing: acceptance. Accept your body as it is and be willing to continue accepting it no matter what.

- **Embrace Your Personality**

Just as your body is unique, so too is your personality. You were uniquely designed to be you, with no one else being exactly as you are. Your personality likely has many quirks and idiosyncrasies that seem "different" when you compare yourself to others. Maybe you snort laugh at the way bunnies hop. Or you have an obsession with reading horror novels and storing them in a weird OCD way. Maybe you cannot stand tomatoes. Maybe you laugh at sad movies, and cry at romantic comedies. All of these different things go in to making you uniquely you.

Rather than attempting to wash away your natural characteristics in favor of being "normal" (which literally does not exist by the way) you should start letting yourself be you. Furthermore, stop censoring yourself for fear of what others think. If you see a great opportunity to crack a joke in the middle of a conversation, let your wit take over.

If you are walking by a bookstore on your first date and you desperately want to go in after seeing a special edition Twilight box set in the window, throw the rules to the wind and go in. Your date's not judging you. I am, but your date isn't. Actually, they may be judging you too. But don't let that stop you. There is no need to stop being you in the presence of other people. Unapologetically embrace you.

• Date Yourself

There is something powerful about taking yourself out on dates. Just as you would go on a date to get to know someone else, take yourself on a date, too. Give yourself the chance to get to know yourself in a way that no one else truly knows you. Go to your favorite restaurant, coffee shop, museum, or other date spot and treat yourself. Purchase the fancier coffee, order the meal you can't pronounce, get your favorite things, and really treat yourself to a no-limits date. Do unto yourself as you would if you were taking someone else out, or how you would want to be treated if someone was taking you out on your very first date together. Do it often.

The more you give yourself the royal treatment that we tend to reserve for others, the more you will feel worthy of your own love, attention, and affection. Do not be afraid to shower yourself in love in all of the ways imaginable. Even if it feels uncomfortable or strange at first, you will soon find that it actually kind of rocks. In fact, it rocks a lot. Soon, you will find that it is easier for you to receive your own love. Then, it will become easier to love the skin you live in. When that happens, being comfortable with yourself comes naturally.

CHAPTER 17:

FEELING BETTER
ONE STEP AT A TIME

No one heals overnight. You hear me? I do not care how many ah-ha moments or quantum leaps you have read about. I know you have read about them, too. If you scroll through social media—even just for a minute—you will likely find some form of material that says: "How I became healthy in 30 days!" "How I got rich in 30 days!" "How I healed my personal trauma in 30 days!" or some other exciting news about how someone just completely turned their life around in a mere few weeks, days, or sometimes even minutes.

Honestly, I want to call it bullshit. That's right, bullshit! No one magically changes their entire lives in just 30 days using extremely vague steps. It just does not happen like that.

Anyone who has experienced seemingly overnight success with something has typically been highly devoted to having that experience manifest into their reality. They have used dedication, perseverance, practice, and skill-development in the background to get themselves to that point. Whether they truly realize it or not, the success they experienced came from a lot more than just thirty days of changes. Those thirty days may have been the thirty with the most notable or noticeable growth, but they certainly do not hold all of the credit for the success that person experienced.

Getting to where you desire to go (in this case, to relaxation and less worry) takes time. There are many steps involved, each of which has its own little set of time that it will take you to accomplish. What may take one person a week could take you a day, and vice versa. It could even take months, or years. Attempting to place deadlines on these things is nonsense. This unrealistic expectation feeds into the illusion that things can be accomplished right now. From a marketing front, it is genius: it appeals to your desire for instant gratification and immediate return environment living. Unfortunately, once enacted, it might just make you feel like a major failure or the anomaly of the universe because what seemed to be working for others in five seconds is not working for you.

Giving yourself some slack and realizing that healing and releasing that worry takes time is essential. You have to be willing to remove the idea that it will happen overnight or any other sense of urgency from your mind. Instead of hoping to reach the end-goal by next week, try focusing on just building positive habits and reaching the next step of feeling better. Consider what one thing could change in your life right now that would have the biggest impact, and work toward that. For example, maybe worrying about your job less would have a major impact on your well-being overall. Then, focus on having less stress surrounding your work.

The old saying goes: "How do you eat an elephant? One bite at a time." This is true for healing and feeling better, too. Taking it just one step at a time and celebrating your success at each step is a far more productive way to get to where you desire to go than attempting to leap to the top from ground zero.

If you have a tendency to find your healing and getting better as a point of stress in and of itself, it may be time to focus on that as your first step. Begin your journey by accepting that it will take you time. Remove the pressure from yourself and allow yourself to have the opportunity to really invest in each step without any rigid expectations on how long that step is going to last or how you are going to feel when you reach it. The more you release the outcome, the easier it is to reach it and the better it feels. It may sound counter intuitive, but it is true.

Here is a great way to understand it. Imagine you are a child and you are learning to play baseball. You are standing with the bat in your hand and the pitcher throws the ball at you. Your coach screams harshly at you, demanding better of you and bullying you any time you fail. Each time you miss, you feel increasingly upset and your stress rises. Soon, you cannot even focus on the ball, so you are missing every single pitch by a longshot. Your coach's attachment to you hitting the ball has resulted in them becoming so controlling that they have actually prevented you from succeeding. Had they calmed down and given you better instruction rather than simply getting angrier and meaner, you would have likely figured it out and hit the ball several times over.

The same goes for you with healing. Every time you bully yourself for not healing better, faster, or with greater results, you are actually holding yourself back. Instead, if you truly feel that you are not reaching your desired goals, slow down and ask yourself why. Giving yourself better instruction on how to achieve your goals will go a lot further than bullying yourself for not achieving them at all.

CHAPTER 18:

PUTTING IT ALL TOGETHER

If you have read until this point, congratulations, this means that there is hope for you. You have a better attention span than most of the people in the digital age, which must mean that you are serious about finding freedom from the chronic worrying that you have subscribed to up until now. By now, maybe you are already using daily practices and incorporating many of the other strategies offered to you throughout this book. Now, you have all of the great ingredients, but it's time to put it all together.

Knowing how to combine all of your best strategies into a realistic plan for minimizing worry and promoting a more stress-free life is important. This requires one very specific skill that you can begin developing right now: self-awareness.

Practicing self-awareness will allow you to become aware of what your needs are in any given moment. This will also support you in understanding what may be running in the background of your mind causing extra stress. Think of your mind as a computer screen and all of your different thoughts as tabs on an internet browser. Your self-awareness gives you the capacity to look at each tab and determine which one needs to be focused on at any given time. It also helps you in recognizing which can be closed, which are causing problems, and which can be dealt with later.

When you practice self-awareness, it becomes a lot easier to serve yourself in a way that minimizes worry and stress. You can quickly become aware of when anxiety or worry is arising, and you can pinpoint what is the likely cause. While some things may have much deeper meanings than you initially thought, having a good idea of what the trigger is can help you determine what your course of action is. Furthermore, being able to determine what type of worry or anxiety you are facing can support you in deciding what course of action is going to be the best to help you overcome it.

Here is an example of what it would look like in your life to put it all together using self-awareness and the strategies within this book.

You are on your way to work when someone runs a red light and nearly swipes your car. Within an instant, anxiety begins to rise within you. You know exactly why because the trigger was obvious, and potentially life-threatening. You breathe through it as you make your way to work, not wanting to be late. By the time you arrive, your worry has faded into the background but has not yet left the scene because you did not feel it through. You go about business as usual, when suddenly the boss's secretary comes into your office and informs you that he wants to talk to you that afternoon.

Curiosity quickly turns to worry as you begin wondering what it could possibly be about. You notice that the rest of the hours between then and your appointment seem to drone on. The time passes slowly, every knock at your door causes you to jump, and you cannot focus on your work because you are so concerned about what the boss could possibly need to talk to you about. Thoughts cross your mind as you rack your brain trying to think of how you may have upset him and what the consequences may be. Will you get fired? Will you be demoted? Will he put you on probation? You cannot remember what you have done or why.

Suddenly, you realize that you are caught in a worry spiral. You recognize it and begin deep breathing.

Then, you grab a piece of paper from your printer and set a timer for five minutes so that you can have some scheduled worry time. You dump out everything on the paper that could have possibly gone wrong and everything that you are worried about. You realize that some of this is residual worry from your experience in the morning that you left unresolved so that you could begin your day. When the timer goes off, you stop. Then, you begin sparking your senses so that you can relax. You spend about five minutes looking, listening, feeling, smelling, and tasting. After, you realize you are feeling much better. So you go on with your day and finish up more work than you had all morning.

Later, when you arrive at your boss's office for him to talk to you, you feel small bouts of panic rising within you again. However, because you have not spent the entire day overwhelmed with worry, you are able to breathe through it. When you sit down in his office to talk, he actually seems cheery. You learn that all he wanted to talk to you about was an upcoming project that you would be involved in. When you leave, you realize that the worry earlier was all for nothing. You had no reason to be worried.

When you arrive home that night, you recognize that your day was a challenge, so you set aside extra time to invest in relaxing. You draw yourself a hot bath, turn on some music, and begin shaking your booty like an extra in a music video before dipping into the warm water to calm down for the evening.

As you can see, having access to supportive tools on a whim can really support you in minimizing anxiety and worry as they arise. Knowing how to relax yourself and feel through emotions immediately, rather than letting them percolate is very important. Even though you will not necessarily get it every time (such as in our previous scenario where you didn't have time to do a brain dump first thing in the morning), you can have your Zen tools on speed dial so you can begin using and easily accessing them in your daily life.

The more you practice incorporating these activities into your life, the easier it becomes for you to nip fear or worry in the bud before it evolves into something much more challenging to face. It also allows you to recognize when you are carrying a large amount of residual tense energy in your body so that you can plan accordingly and destress following a particularly challenging day. Ideally, the more challenging of a day you have had, the more you should invest in your wind-down at the end of the day.

But, know where to draw the line and recognize the truth. If after work you head home, pop on Netflix and binge watch it every single night, you may feel as though you are winding down, but in reality, what you are probably doing is avoiding dealing with your emotions. As a result, you'll just end up retaining that residual stressful energy and struggling to relax when any more stress is added to the pile. Knowing how to turn it down and relax is important, but knowing when and how much is also necessary. In order to begin practicing de-stressing in your own life, make sure that you are actively practicing self-awareness and using it as the means by which you determine what tool you need to use to minimize your crazy feelings.

CHAPTER 19:

NEVER LOOK BACK

You're turning over a new leaf now. But how do you keep it that way? Being able to keep yourself in line when you are learning something new is a real feat. Seriously, it takes a lot of discipline and determination to ensure that you are staying on track with your goals and not falling behind or jumping off the wagon altogether. If you tend to be the type of person who struggles to stay on track with new goals (also known as "being a human"), this chapter will support you in finding ways that you can stay on track to prevent you from falling behind or giving up on yourself before you really have a chance to make any significant changes.

Here is what you need to do: identify your likely problems in advance, create a plan, check in with yourself often, and be honest. Doing these things will ensure that you set yourself up for success and that you have no reason to worry that you will not be able to achieve your goal of being less worried. Seriously, I mean it. Even if you have never really stayed on track with a goal to date, you still have hope. I believe in you. Let's break things down a little bit further:

- **Identify And Plan For Likely Problems In Advance**

Recognizing what your weaknesses are is key. Being able to identify what limits you and understanding how these limitations impact you can support you in doing better at this whole human being thing. Having a belief that you are going to decide to do better and then genuinely believing that just because you said so you will never make a mistake again is naive. Instead, you need to realize that the weaknesses you face today will continue to be your weaknesses tomorrow. That is, unless you plan for them and do something about them. That way they can be offset, and you can continue to succeed in spite of these weaknesses.

For example, say you want to work out after the gym every day, but instead you go home and binge watch Hulu all night because you are invested in a new show. "When this one is done, I'll start!" you lie to yourself, genuinely believing that you might. Instead of letting this hold you back time and again, cancel your Hulu subscription until you change your ways. Right? Simple. If the idea of doing this makes your head spin around in circles and your body curl into the fetal position, twitching with involuntary convulsions, you definitely need to cancel that Hulu subscription. Remove your potential success barriers and make a game plan in order to achieve your ultimate goal—in this case, not being a total stress ball.

Similarly, you can apply this to the issue of worry. Instead of believing that suddenly you will never worry when say, a deadline fast approaches, believe that you will and create a plan for what you will do when the worry starts. Have an idea in action as to how you are going to go ahead and release this worry so that you can stay focused on the task at hand and complete your goal before deadline.

- **Plan To Fail, Many Times**

I know this may not sound like the best "self-help" advice, but no one, no matter who you are, will work toward a goal and not experience some degree of failure at least once. Maybe much more. Getting things right the first time just ain't a thing.

If it were, you would never have picked up this book because there would be no need for it.

Instead of avoiding the fact that you will fail many times, face it. Early. As you are setting your goal in motion, also set a plan for what you will do to overcome any failure that arises. This way, rather than wasting time being trapped in your failure and setting false goals that you are going to do better in the future, you already have something to fall back on. You already know what part of the plan to execute when failure arises, so all you have left to do is execute it.

This can be especially helpful during these moments of weakness when we naturally begin to bully ourselves for how badly we have done. Eventually, that nasty bully in your mind will learn to zip it. But until then, you need to plan for it to be obnoxiously loud and even more obnoxious in the face of your failure. That way you can be certain that any time something negative begins you can say "Nope, I already knew this would happen! Here's what I am going to do about it!" And then you can move on unscathed.

- **Be Brutally Honest When You Check In**

Being overly modest when you check in with yourself will not support you in staying in line. You need to be so honest with yourself that there is nowhere for you to run or hide. Pretending that you have been doing better than you have will not support you in finding answers or getting to where you need to go. Instead, it will only support you in staying in denial about how bad things really are for you during times of serious misery.

Everything you do in pursuit of this goal to eliminate worry and stress should be brutally honest. When you do brain dumps, make sure that you are honest about why you are worried and what you are worried about, even if the worries make zero sense or seem to be way larger than anything that would reasonably happen. The more honest you are, the more you can understand where your worries come from and how they impact you.

If when you are checking in you realize that you have not been doing as well as you thought at managing your anxiety, admit it. If you realize you are doing better, celebrate it. Do not be modest in either direction. The more honest you are, the better you can focus on your solutions and you can get a measure of what needs to be done to improve from where ever you are at that moment. The only person judging here is you, so turn that nasty voice down and get real with yourself.

- **Get To The Root**

Following in line with the same note as before, get down to the root of things. Nothing will derail you faster than a hidden land mine. Having something major going on in the background that you are not addressing will have you feeling like you are going crazy every time some anxiety or worry pops up, but in reality, what is actually happening is that you are being entrapped by a major emotion or concern that has been left unaddressed.

When you are finding yourself over-the-top worried, take some time to sit with your worry and get deeper into what is bugging you. Follow your worries all the way down to the root, then start with relaxing the root cause and healing it. This will ensure that there is nothing lingering in the background, hijacking your success by keeping you in a chronic state of underlying anxiety and worry.

- **Realize That Even Small Advancements Are Huge**

We have a crazy addiction to chastising ourselves when we do not achieve the exact level of success that we desire to achieve by a specific time and date. While this criticism may be somewhat reasonable with goals that are actually measurable, when it comes to something like easing worry, you need to go easier on yourself. Punishing yourself for worrying more than you feel is necessary will only result in further worry and stress. In the end, you will give up on your personal peace goals because they will feel unachievable.

Success, instead, will come from realizing that first, healing emotions is not really a measurable goal. So, when it comes to matters like this, let go of the rigid unachievable goals, and set ones that are more accommodating and able to account for what you are likely going to be able to achieve. Do not get overly specific. For example, instead of saying "I will completely love my job in three months" say "I will feel less stress around work in three months." Then work steadily toward this goal.

When you take away your attachment to the outcome by removing expectations on how it will feel, you give yourself the opportunity to stay focused on the tangible task in front of you. This means that you can measure the bits that actually are measurable, and the way you feel will come naturally as a byproduct. Otherwise, you will just worry because you do not feel the way you expected you would, which is obviously counter intuitive to the whole not worrying thing.

- **Forgive Yourself In Advance**

Far too many precious minutes have been wasted in people's lives with bullying themselves around for not achieving their desires right away. If and when you experience a mistake, hang up, setback, or otherwise, forgive yourself. Matter of fact, go ahead and forgive yourself in advance. Being willing to admit that not everything is going to run smoothly and that you are not going to fully succeed right off the bat is the way to go. Forgiving yourself in advance means that when you have one of those setbacks and that inner mean girl inevitably starts bullying you for it, you can come back and say "No, because I accept myself and I forgive myself."

Forgiving yourself in advance is not throwing in the white flag and deciding that there is no way you will ever be able to be anything other than a perpetually freaked out spaz. Instead, it is realizing that you will experience some degree of failure on your road to your "chill out" goal, and that by recognizing and honoring this failure you give yourself permission to stay working toward your goal, rather than getting wrapped up in guilt, and getting hung up on the different things that are set in your path to distract you and pull you off the path of success.

- **Set Reminders**

Unfortunately, with something like worry there is no way to predict exactly when it is going to strike. Keeping reminders placed around your house on sticky notes, setting intermittent messages and personal check in alerts on your phone, and having a friend check in on you are all great ways to help you remember to check in with yourself and stay focused on the end-goal. Soon enough, you will achieve it.

Keeping yourself in line is not as easy as it sounds, but it is necessary. If you go into your goal setting with the immediate knowledge that you are not going to succeed right away because of the many failures you will endure, it is a lot easier to stay on track. Isn't that ironic—accepting failure will make it easier for you to succeed. This is because you anticipate the setbacks. Therefore, they do not cause uncertainty and guilt which can cause an intense spiral of worry, anxiety, shame, self-deprecation, and other painful and challenging emotions.

If you keep yourself in line long enough, you can guarantee that you will experience great success using these strategies. Changing your life is possible and misery can be healed. Give yourself a chance.

CONCLUSION

Thank you for reading to the end (Yes, I'm sorry it's over). By now, you (should) have learned why it is so important for your health and sanity to avoid negativity, worry, and fear, and how to employ the techniques in this book to get over it. I hope now you've grown a set and can handle your life better. That seems like a good note to end on, but we'll go a little further in wrapping things up and summarizing what we've learned.

Being able to recognize anxiety and worry for what they are, and understanding why they exist in your biology is the beginning of understanding why you freak out so often. It also makes sense as to why you struggle to recover easily from freak outs and chronic stress: because you are literally wired to experience it. Knowing that makes a world of difference, because it means that you don't have to sit around wondering why you cannot seem to get your shit together. You already know—you are wired to fail. And now you have the solutions you need to rewire yourself to succeed.

The next step for you is to get on track. If you have been on and off the wagon since starting this book, consider that your grace period. Realize that it takes time to learn and integrate all these knowledge bombs, and that you are allowed to have a period of orienting yourself and figuring out how to nail down these tactics within your own life.

Begin integrating these tactics by incorporating things like set worry times, sensory relaxation, and playing pretend to help get the worry out of your mind. Realize it may take quite some time to fully reach a state of relaxation because of how much stress you have been carrying with you. But, once you kick that stress's ass right out the door, you will have a much easier time recognizing it, using it for its biological purpose, and then releasing it from your body so that you can return to having a greater sense of calmness in your life.

If you find that you are struggling, make sure you stay focused on your staying-in-line plan. Keep it sharp, useful, and available so that you know exactly what you need to do if you fall off the wagon. You may even benefit from having it written in a note on your phone so that if you are on the go when it happens, you can hop into your note, read it, and gain inspiration on what to do next to ensure that you do not waste any time feeling sorry for yourself about your emotional setback.

And that, my friend, is all she wrote. Best of luck on your journey to personal inner peace. And if ever you have a moment where you feel like everything is falling apart around you and you've already taken a hot bath, sniffed candles, walked sideways, and kidnapped a stranger's child to play make-believe with, and you still feel hopelessly unable to pull yourself together and act like an emotionally stable person, imagine my voice in your head telling you: You. Can Frickin. Do It.

If at any point in this book you learned something, smiled, nodded, or chuckled, please leave a review on Amazon letting us know why you loved this book!

And be sure to check out my other ebooks, paperback books, and audiobooks on Amazon and Audible!

Like what you just read?
Sad it's over?
Turn that frown upside down
and listen to the audiobook
(~~usually $14.95~~)
for **FREE**.

Search for my name
"Reese Owen" on Audible.

Audible member? Use a credit.
New to Audible? Get this audiobook **free**
with your free trial.

ALL BOOKS BY REESE OWEN

Check out my other ebooks,
paperback books, and audiobooks
available on Amazon and Audible:

B*tch Don't Kill My Vibe
How To Stop Worrying, End Negative Thinking,
Cultivate Positive Thoughts,
And Start Living Your Best Life

Just Do The Damn Thing
How To Sit Your @ss Down Long Enough To
Exert Willpower, Develop Self Discipline,
Stop Procrastinating, Increase Productivity,
And Get Sh!t Done

Make Your Brain Your B*tch
Mental Toughness Secrets To Rewire Your Mindset
To Be Resilient And Relentless, Have Self Confidence
In Everything You Do,
And Become The Badass You Truly Are